£4.95

G000093288

WARTIME M
A COLLECTION OF PERSONAL
MEMORIES
OF THE SECOND WORLD WAR

EDITED
BY
Doris E. Pullen

Distributor: Able Publishing Services
13 Station Road, Knebworth, Herts, SG3 6AP.UK
Tel: 01438 812320   Fax 01438 815232

By the same author:
Sydenham
Penge
Forest Hill
Dulwich
Beckenham

To
MY CHILDREN

Reprinted by Triographics, Knebworth, Herts
1995

Contents

Preface

The inception of a book of memories

Some time ago I felt a strong urge to gather material on the 1939-45 war —
one which I had lived through myself — and so I decided to ask various
people I knew if they would kindly allow me to publish some of their personal
stories. Many of them replied that they felt sure that nothing they could
remember would be of the slightest interest to anyone, and others said, "What
a good idea!" and promptly proceeded to write out their memoirs.
Consequently, small articles have been coming in to me all the year, and now
there are enough compiled to make a book.

I wish to thank the contributors — my husband G.V.R. (John) Pullen,
my cousin George Holley, and my friends Josephine Birchenough, Muriel V.
Searle, Brigadier C.E.F. Turner, Iain Orr, Air Commodore N. Hyde, C.T.
Randall, John Sheppard, Eric Lukeman, G. Evans, Lydia White, I.
Cropper, Olive Ainge, and Lewis Blake for allowing me to use their very
individual experiences. Especially I must thank my good friend Edna
Antrobus who not only wrote a chapter but also typed up some of the
manuscript, and Frederick Whyler who edited the text; without their
encouragement and help I would not have succeeded in producing these
memories for others to read.

The snippets taken from newspapers show events that were occurring at
the beginning of the war, and again during the last weeks. I felt these stories
might give the readers an idea of life as it was then, and they would see how
there was no escape for the ordinary 'man in the street'. We were dragged into
the war and everybody had to play their part and make the best of it. I hope
the feeling that we did not really want to fight comes through, but when the
country is at war, we faced up to situations we certainly did not like. It was not
easy, but we lived through it and thanked God when it was over. So this book
of memories is produced 'forty years on', with the object of spreading hope in
a depressed world.

Doris E. Pullen, 1985

The First Days of War

Items picked out from **The Times** *newspaper, 1 — 7 September 1939*

1st September 1939

Mr Herbert Morrison, the Leader of the London County Council and Chairman of the Air Raid Precaution (ARP) Committee, delivered a message to all Londoners. The children were told to be prepared to be taken into the country areas and would have to leave their parents. 500,000 children were to be evacuated from the London schools and this was to be a combined effort of trains, buses and any other method of transport, to enable the young to be taken to a place of safety.

The Minister of Health, Mr Elliott, said that the Prime Minister (PM) had especially asked him to make it quite clear that evacuation did not mean that war was inevitable, only a possibility. The nation's motto was to be 'Stand to your posts, be prepared, and do your duty'.

The Lord Privy Seal Department issued information for the benefit of the public for their protection and hints on how to deal with bombs in an air raid. It could be assumed that if a small bomb or even fifty of them fell within a square mile, any individual would have a 100 to 1 chance of escaping alive. Anderson shelters properly earthed over would be safe except from a direct hit. Even an ordinary dwelling-house could supply a good deal of protection, especially if a person was sheltering in a passage or a basement room. The glass and windows should be covered with tape criss-cross fashion to prevent splinters flying, and if the air raid warning was heard, take cover immediately.

The overseas telephone services were cut off and telegrams sent must bear the name and address of the sender, for security reasons. Careless talk cost lives. We were to be careful.

Instructions were issued to all men who were in the Reserve forces of the Navy, Army or Air Force, to proceed to their depots at once and report for duty. They were to bring their uniforms if they had them. All organizations cancelled their social engagements and the country prepared for war.

The Japanese organized a Day of Prayer for the Prosperity of the Japanese Empire and all the people were order to bow in the direction of the Imperial Palace at a given time.

The Moscow Pact was ratified. A non-aggression pact between the Soviet Union and Germany had been signed in Moscow on 24th August by Mr Molotov and Herr von Ribbentrop and it was to last for ten years. A New

Conscription Bill was submitted by the Russian Commissar of Defence, Marshal Voroshinov and passed to conscript all men of 18 and 19.

The Pope appealed for peace, and the Polish people said they were ready for negotiations. The whole of Europe was very uneasy and the eyes of the world were on Germany and Great Britain.

High in the sky the planets of Mars and Jupiter were prominent. Astrologers were remarking upon the positioning of the stars — they were placed ready for war.

2nd September 1939

According to Adolf Hitler, Germany had no wish to go to war but they were not prepared to put force aside. They marched into Poland and hoisted the Swastika flag — the twisted cross — over the city of Danzig and stated that they had liberated the Polish people by returning them to the Fatherland — despite the wish of the majority to stay free.

Poland was invaded and bombed at 5.30 a.m. on the 1st September without any warning and by the next day, Neville Chamberlain, the Prime Minister of Great Britain, announced that we must keep our promise to Poland, our Allies, to take up arms against the enemy.

3rd September 1939

A State of War existed between His Majesty, George VI, and Germany from 11 a.m. on 3rd September 1939. At 9 a.m. H.M.'s Ambassador in Berlin addressed a communication to the German Government saying that unless they were prepared to give H.M. Government in the United Kingdom a satisfactory assurance that the German Government had suspended all the aggressive action against Poland and be prepared to withdraw their forces from Polish territory, we should have to fulfil our obligation to Poland and fight. No such assurance was received, so from that moment onwards, the British nation was at war.

4th September 1939

The London Zoo was closed. All the poisonous snakes and insects were destroyed for safety reasons. Many animals were taken to the vets to be put to sleep kindly, rather than let them suffer pain and fear. Places of entertainment were closed and the London shops almost ran out of food as people stocked up for a seige. Gas masks were issued for babies, and mothers were told to carry them at all times on the bottom of the pram.

King George VI broadcast to his people and a War Cabinet was set up. Lord Gort was appointed Commander-in-Chief of the British forces. Suddenly the country seemed to be flooded with men in uniforms and the men became heroes. Ten Bills were hurriedly passed in one day through Parliament and the result of one of these was to ration fuel and petrol. Motorists had to paint the mudguards of their cars white so they could be seen in the dark, and the lights on the cars were covered, with only a small slit left visible. No lights were allowed to shine from open doors or windows and black-out restrictions had to be rigidly enforced.

The Canadian Prime Minister, Mr Mackenzie King, broadcast to the nation from Ottawa to say that Canada would support Britain in any way they could and the men over there were queueing up to volunteer for the forces. The Canadians wanted to come over right away to help the Mother country.

The first British ship to be sunk was the *Athenia* sailing with 1,400 passengers off the Hebrides. It was torpedoed without warning and many lives were lost. War had started and ended already for some.

5th September 1939

The RAF dropped 6,000,000 leaflets over Germany explaining to the German people why we had gone to war. Our planes returned safely and they seemed to have given the Luftwaffe a surprise as they had not expected the British to venture quite so far over their territory on the second day of war. The leaflets could have been bombs.

650,000 children and infirm adults were evacuated successfully from London, and recruiting depots were crowded with young men enlisting with the Armed Services, willing to fight for country and King. Across the world the Australians were joining in their thousands and 78,000 men were called up during the first week of war.

Business in London was at a standstill and for once the Stock Exchange remained closed.

6th September 1939

King George VI and Queen Elizabeth took on numerous public duties. They visited and inspected the Civil Defence Units, speaking to as many people as they could, and were obviously keen to find out for themselves how Britain intended to defend herself. They showed great concern for their people.

Queen Elizabeth went on to visit the Red Cross Headquarters. Her kindly eyes showed her sympathy and the people loved her. The Royal Family set their standards high and the country prepared to follow them.

President Roosevelt proclaimed America's neutrality, although most people in this country knew that the Americans would step in to help if they thought we could not handle the battle alone. We were very conscious that they were our 'big brothers' and they would keep a watchful eye on our progress.

The Rhodesian men volunteered and so did the Australians and the New Zealanders. The Fiji Islanders very loyally placed themselves and all that they had, at the disposal of the King of Great Britain. Portugal stood by us, India rallied to the call, and Nepal offered to send 8,000 troops.

Yugoslavia, Argentine and Chile remained neutral and General Franco ordered all Spaniards to stay out of the war. France was automatically in the war with us and so were the Netherlands, Belgium, Latvia and Estonia. The French Maginot Line was the first line of defence and it was thought to be quite strong enough to withstand the assault of the German Army. Sadly this was not so.

7th September 1939

Enemy planes were turned back by British fighters when they approached the east coast. This was in the first days of war when so much was expected of so few. Our comparatively untrained men had to become very skilled fighters in the shortest possible time, giving all the strength they could muster in the effort to beat off the attackers.

Even peaceful Mahatma Ghandi remarked, "What will life be worth if England and France fall? Hitler knows no God but brute force and Mr Chamberlain says he will listen to nothing else." Gandhi recognized the fact that Great Britain was forced to stand for what she believed to be right, against the powers of evil, and as so many of the Indian people were drawn into the war, he must have felt very sad at heart as he was unable to prevent it by using peaceful, non-combatant means.

By the end of the first week of war, the Stock Exchange had reopened and so had the cinemas and a few places of entertainment. Life went on as normally as possible whilst the people trained themselves for resisting attack. They learned to manage without luxuries on minimum allowances of food, using coupons for fair allocation and putting on as brave a face as possible to reduce anxiety and to help the men at the front and so keep England free. They did not know then that the war was to last six long years.

Memories of the Years 1939-45

by Doris E. Pullen

It is not easy to cast my mind back forty-five years to the first days of the war, now in 1985. I was married on 29th July 1939 at St. Bartholomew's Church, Sydenham, and the few months of my early married life seemed somewhat chaotic and depressing. I lived in a flat in my mother's house; it didn't seem worth while moving into a house of my own because the war was coming. We all felt that war was inevitable after Neville Chamberlain had returned from Munich with his useless piece of paper, signed by Hitler. No one trusted the pact or believed Hitler really wanted peace, but it gave us a breathing space to prepare for the war to come, for which we were totally unprepared in 1938. My father, a regular serviceman in the RAF, came home with tales of men having to stand on guard armed with long staves instead of rifles. He had no idea how he was meant to tackle the enemy if they suddenly dropped from the sky, with just a long stick — but he had his own views on this!

At that period of time I was a private hairdresser, visiting 'ladies' at home, washing their hair and curling it, either on tight curlers or heated irons. I would act as 'lady's-maid', getting 'Madam' dressed and ready for a glamorous evening out for 10/- (50p). This was good money then. One of my best clients was a Mrs ffoukes (2 small fs) of Bishopsthorpe Road. I would sometimes visit her three times a week, to dress out her 'coiffure' for 1/6d a session. It often took me half an hour, and she was very particular. She *never* combed her own hair.

It was during one of my visits to her house that the war started for me. I was doing her hair in her special private air raid shelter when some of the first bombs in South London fell on Sydenham, in Earlsthorpe Road. The Germans had attacked, and a string of small bombs was jettisoned, whistling down and causing several explosions, which did minor damage to the houses around. Glass blew out and holes appeared in roof-tops as slates fell off. I finished Mrs ffoukes's hair and walked home, stepping over rubble, to see if there had been any damage to our house, 66 Newlands Park, and thankfully it was all right this time — no damage for us — so we could carry on.

My husband was soon called up into the RAF and so was my brother. All the men I knew gradually went into the forces. Many did not return.

I joined my husband at Weston-super-Mare where he was stationed and I

11

lived in the village of Locking with an elderly couple. It was at the dances in the Weston Pavilion that I met several of the TTs (Tee and Tyneside soldiers) who were training there ready for the battle of El Alamein. During the day I worked in the hospital on the Air Force camp as a VAD and dealt mainly with men sick with minor ailments.

After training at Locking, my husband was posted to Stroud in Gloustershire for a few weeks and then back to Heston in Middlesex, after which he was posted to South Africa for a couple of years. By this time I had two little girls and my life had altered. I had tried being evacuated to Wales and found I was not wanted, so I had moved back into my old home in Newlands Park, Sydenham. I lived there until 1944 after my second daughter was born, but when she was about 4 months old the flying bombs started so I evacuated again. It was fortunate for me that I was away when the house was blasted beyond repair by a flying bomb falling in the garden, then I could not go home any more.

A house was requisitioned by the council for us in Bishopsthorpe Road and my mother, aunt and I lived there until the end of the war. My husband returned home and I felt it was very unfair to be a burden to my mother any longer. She had been marvellous putting up with me and my children for so long, which could not have been easy for her.

My wartime experiences as an evacuee were traumatic. I found that I really wasn't wanted by anyone as I had two babies — one perhaps would have been bearable but not two. I had tried to live in South Wales for a while when my second baby was very small, but this was a disaster. My landlady could not stand nappies being dried in front of the fire — there were no electrical heaters or spin driers in those days. The clothes had to hang in front of a coal fire to dry with direct heat, or be put around the gas stove. It was difficult.

My journey to Wales, however, was quite interesting. My mother and I tried to board the train at Paddington Station but couldn't, as it seemed to be full. One of the porters, after receiving a tip, said, "Follow me, Ma'am — I'll find you a seat," which he did. My mother and I and my two babies, were pushed into an almost empty compartment at the front of the train with a man and woman in it. The money paid off. We had the comfort of a 1st class compartment and a seat.

I thought the woman was 'different' and the man certainly had an air of authority about him. We had chocolates (a luxury) which we shared with them and I fed my baby, hiding my chest modestly with a shawl draped around my shoulders as it was not decent to expose one's body to strangers, and they tactfully did not seem to notice when the baby cried and had to be fed. My little girl sat on the lady's lap, and we talked amicably, but she did not seem to know much about young children.

At Badminton the train made a special stop and the porters and station-master, resplendent in his gold-braided cap, lined up outside the carriage door . Our travelling companions prepared to get out and the aristocratic lady said to my mother, "If you want help, my dear, let me know. Come to the Hall because we have plenty of rooms." She was the Duchess of Beaufort, and he was the Duke, Master of the King's Horse — both very charming people and very kind. No wonder we felt they were slightly different! But they couldn't have been more friendly to my mother and me on that long train journey.

My father, who was the Station Warrant Officer at St Athan aerodrome, was George Ernest Lord, 17168. He had been in the forces since he joined the Royal Flying Corps in 1917 and had already served twenty-three years with the Royal Air Force. My mother sometimes rented a room near the camp and he would stay with her for a while. She had taken accommodation at Cowbridge in South Wales to be near him and it was to this house I ventured from London as an evacuee.

The train arrived at the station late at night and everywhere was pitch black. No lights could be seen anywhere in the black-out. My father, however, was there to meet us and we trundled back with all our luggage, two very tired women, a child of two and baby one month old. I think it was one of my worst experiences of the war — trying to sleep in the bitterly cold bedroom, lit by a small candle, with a crying baby I couldn't feed because my milk had stopped. Mother and I just walked her up and down all night trying to pacify her with a dummy. We were frozen with cold and very miserable. My father had returned to camp and there we were alone — all I wanted to do was to go back home as I felt the bombing was preferable to this uncomfortable misery.

As my trip to Cowbridge was such a complete disaster, I soon returned to London. I could not take the Duchess up on her generous offer because I felt she might have regretted it. Babies are not easy, as they cry and two-year-olds do make a mess. How we survived, despite the attempts of the Germans to kill us, I shall never know, but survive we did.

In London, we slept under the Morrison steel table shelter for a while, but luckily I was away at St Albans in Hertfordshire, staying with friends, when the house was bombed. I had returned home when the V2 rockets started. From then onwards, we could sleep in our beds again. There was less nervous strain with a rocket, for it you heard it, it had missed you, and you were all right. If it had hit you, you wouldn't have heard it at all. You would probably be dead, so what was the use of taking shelter? You couldn't wait all day for the bomb to drop on you, so we just carried on as normally as possible.

'Normal' then was queuing for food, cooking with 'ersatz' foods — for we had very little milk, cheese, butter or sugar, and a minimum amount of meat and fish — but we managed. Clothes were on coupons, so we could not buy very many clothes. Stockings could only be bought on the 'black market' but the troops sent silk ones over in letters from abroad and they were resold over here. We did not look very fashionable but it did not matter as we didn't go far.

We couldn't go anywhere and no one cared. We were all in the same boat together. We slept when we could so that we maintained strength to carry on. We were determined to live. The Germans were not going to beat us!

I know I did not expect to come through the war — so when we heard a big bomb had been dropped on Hiroshima, I did not feel any particular disgust, as I hoped that this meant the end of the war for us. After all, we had been on the other end of bombing raids for quite a long while. I did not feel it was any worse for the enemy to die than it was for our people. Living in wartime makes you less sensitive to others.

We may not have seen our civilians burned in such large numbers all at once, but we had seen individuals burned, maimed and killed and for each person who dies, or is injured, I expect it feels much the same and just as terrible for each one of them.

It was a wonderful relief to feel we might soon be able to sleep safely at night and the men would be able to return home, though for me, as I had not had a man around for so long, I did not particularly want my husband back. Sounds rotten, but I had 'grown up' whilst he was away and I was not the girl he left behind. We had both changed considerably through our various war experiences and we never 'picked up the pieces' together again properly. We were strangers to each other.

In a few years after his return we were divorced and we both started new lives with other people.

The price I paid for living during the war days was high in the loss of some of my more gentle and softer feelings. Perhaps it happens to everyone when they are growing up but I became tougher and harder and stopped being sentimental. We had to enjoy the moment and not bank on having any future. If we lived through it, we considered ourselves lucky but we were changed by our experiences. Our characters were altered by the war and somehow life would never be the same.

It was during the year before the 1939 war started, I began to train as a nurse with the Red Cross. A local unit had been formed under Miss Bennett, the Commandant, in Lawrie Park Road and classes were held in her house on one evening a week. I think the class was about 20 girls strong and we were lectured by a doctor or State Registered Nurse. Sometimes we went to Dr Barnes's house at the other end of Lawrie Park Road, Sydenham, when he was taking the lecture.

I learned the rudiments of First Aid — how to bandage wounds and put splints on broken legs. We stuck injection needles into oranges but this was easier to do than injecting into live flesh as I discovered later. We answered questions and finally sat our exams at the Forest Hill baths which acted as a large local hall. I gained my first certificate and felt very proud of myself.

Next step was actually to work in a hospital. I was eighteen at the time, very naïve and green and easily embarrassed by a naked body. I presented myself to the Lewisham Hospital — a very new girl — to be interviewed by the Matron, and she decided when I would start. We did not receive any money for this — it was all voluntary and we had to supply our own uniform and pay our fares. By the time I was trained and ready, the war had actually started. We had had our baptism of fire and Sydenham had been bombed. Lewisham Hospital was dealing with air raid casualties and I began my part-time nursing career by being plunged in at the deep end — straight into the men's ward.

I remember reporting one Monday morning in my brand new uniform, the 'hat', a standard 'handkerchief' wound around my head, fanning out at the back, with the red cross in the middle directly over my nose. My curly hair poked out in the front because I thought it looked more glamorous that way but this was not to last, as the Sister took one look at me and said, "Push all that hair under you cap Nurse, it's not allowed." So I obediently poked it back.

My white stiffly-starched apron would have stood up on its own. The navy belt gripped me around my waist, the pale blue cotton dress showed I was a novice and a very low-ranking orderly.

The first nursing job I had to do was in B.3 — the male surgical ward — where I was given orders to bath the man in the end bed. I doubt if that poor man had ever had a bath like the one I gave to him. I was scared stiff — I had to remove his pyjamas and strip him down and I washed him delicately without even looking at him — almost with my eyes shut I would think. He did not know that I was so inexperienced, or at least I was not meant to let him know this! I wonder now who he was?

Next call from the Sister was to help a nurse lay out a dead body. This didn't feel quite so bad, because the poor old man could neither feel anything, nor see my discomfort. In those days all holes in the body were plugged with cotton wool — up the nostrils, in the mouth and ears and down to the other extremities. I felt very glad he was dead as I watched the competent nurse doing her job!

Clips being removed from surgical wounds and wiping up, was my next shock — I had never seen great cuts gaping before, nor had I seen colostomies where the bowel contents were brought through the stomach, and into a bag. The stench was pretty horrible, and I felt decidedly sick.

The old men continually called for bottles to relieve themselves, and bed pans were dished out regularly. The pan was removed, covered with a cloth and carried up to the sluice. I found the whole performance of being a nurse entirely repugnant to my nature, as I had previously visualized this work as a gentle stroking of the head with a damp cloth, or holding a patient's hand — not doing the actual 'nitty gritty' and revolting work that a nurse has to do, day after day, without respite, because there is always another person in need of her skill.

The second week I was sent to a women's ward and that was even worse than the men's! There were, so it seemed to me, hundreds of pads to be changed and the women enjoyed being waited on, so they kept you on the run if they could. They were always wanting attention.

The operations were not pleasant. In the ward I was in they were all 'down below' — and so women had to be shaved before the operation. I remember one poor soul very clearly who screamed her head off when the razor approached her, not in my hands I was thankful to say, but I had to hold her down so that she could not move.

She went off to the operating theatre desperately unhappy. No doubt she recovered, but I did not see her again as I had moved on. We nurses were continually moved from ward to ward, wherever a pair of hands were needed or when someone was away on leave or sick.

I did go down to the operating theatre several times. A patient would say to me, "I'll be all right nurse, if you are with me," and I would accompany them as the trolley was wheeled along the cold corridors and down in the lift; I held their hands and felt absolutely terrible.

After they had a 'jab' in the room adjoining the theatre I would wait for them to go unconscious, then go into the theatre with them, wearing a green overall and mask on my face, my hair pinned back under a green hat. It was always so hot in the theatre it was hard to breathe.

I never did see a whole operation. I always had to get myself out before I collapsed. The sight of a woman with her legs strapped up in the air, with the appearance of a trussed chicken, whilst a woman surgeon thrust her hand up inside her as if removing the giblets, will be with me until my dying day, and has left me with a fear and absolute dread of surgery — and hospitals too for that matter.

I came home from my war work feeling physically ill and sick every day and much as I wanted to, I could not admit to cowardly behaviour by giving in, so I had to stick it out.

The Outpatients' Department was quite fun. People came in there for dressings and small things and were not terribly ill — they walked out cheerfully after treatment.

I believe I must have fallen for one of the old gags that they probably tried out on new nurses. I was told to strip a woman off one day and sit her behind the screen in a cubicle. She seemed rather surprised when I asked her to remove all her clothes, but being an obedient soul, she did as she was told. There she was sitting like a rotund Buddha in all her glory when the young doctor arrived to attend to her. His face was quite a picture and his eyes opened wide when he saw her — he had simply come to look at her big toe and the stripping was quite unnecessary! He looked at her feet — I re-dressed her and nothing was ever said about her nakedness. I reckoned I'd fallen for a big joke! I would presume that this poor woman is dead by now but if she ever reads this, I hope she will find it in her heart to forgive me.

All these tales of course relate to wartime hospital life but no doubt nurses still fall into the traps set for new girls.

Back to the days during the war; I must continue. In 1940 I was allocated to work in the old school building in Anerley Road. Part of this house was taken over by the Red Cross for refugees and it was whilst working in a makeshift ward there I saw my first bullet wound — a clean hole through an arm — and I swabbed it gently and stuck on the dressing.

There were many women and children brought over here from France and Belgium in the early days of the war. We had to delouse some of the children, and mainly amuse them by playing games with them, but they were not ill. Some of the women were just suffering from exhaustion, so they slept it off. It was quite a pleasant job as there was no really dirty nursing. They looked after themselves for toilet and bathing and seemed very pleased to be away from the fighting zone. The Germans had advanced to the coast and beaten us back to Dunkirk by this time. Only the Channel separated us from our enemy and we felt they might soon advance over here.

By this time I had become hardened off a little and had learned to recognize the signs of real sickness, especially after seeing one or two people pass away in death. We were suffering from air raids and bombing attacks. My one fear was when returning home after duty dressed in my nurse's uniform, that I would be called upon to assist at some accident or take charge during an air raid, because although I looked efficient, I certainly did not feel it. I was terrified that I should have to organize others when I felt I knew so little. Had I not been in uniform, I would not have worried so much — it was wearing the VAD gear that made me scared.

At the latter part of 1940 I had moved to be near my husband stationed at the RAF camp at Locking, Weston-super-Mare, where I stayed for about six months. I lived in lodgings in the village and worked in the camp during the day. Nursing in the RAF hospital was again different to nursing in Lewisham Hospital or the Refugee Centre. It was full of men sick with bronchitis and bad chests. I painted throats with mauve liquid and swabbed up with disinfectant. These patients soon recovered and were sent home on leave. No one died whilst I was there, but I did catch a chest infection myself and had to give up as I was ill. This actually did prove to be my last appointment as a VAD nurse as I was pregnant and had to resign. However my nursing experiences came in handy when I became a mother. I found I could tackle some of the jobs I had to do for my children with better grace then I should have done without the small amount of medical knowledge that I had gained. My training had given me a certain amount of confidence and for that I was grateful.

At times I had to nurse my sick children. One had meningitis and one was run over and badly injured. Once I had three of them down with chicken-pox altogether — that was a nightmare — and then they all had the usual ailments such as measles, whooping-cough, mumps, coughs and colds and even scarlatina. There was always someone sickening for something out of my brood. I wouldn't want to go through any of those years again. It wasn't easy bringing children up during the war and I was glad when that part of my life ended.

I do not look back at my young life with any feeling of pleasure — it was too traumatic and hard. There was always so much work to do and people to look after. So many mouths to feed and so often, parents went without. No — it wasn't a happy time.

Doris Pullen as a nurse during the war.

Seven Long Years in the Army

by G.V.R. 'John' Pullen

The war had started, and being a young man of twenty I knew I was due to be called up for war service! There was no question of getting out of it, as conscription meant that all men of the age group of 19-21 were to be the first to go. I had been married at St. John's Church Penge in 1939, just before the start of the war, and my wife and I were living in Blandford Road, Beckenham in a little house.

I did not want to go; I was quite happy working in a small shop and returning home to a peaceful life. I wasn't an aggressive boy, and I certainly didn't like fighting.

A telegram arrived one day through the letter box and I knew this meant the end of my particular pattern of life for a while. My first shock was to come; I had to report at Devizes in Wiltshire by 9 a.m. one Thursday morning, and that meant a very early start.

I left home a 'boy' in my best suit, with my suitcase in my hand, full of 'bits and pieces' which I had decided to take with me, soap, flannel, sewing kit, pyjamas, and a few personal photographs.

It is hard to find words to describe one's emotions starting out on a completely new life, and moving out into the unknown full of apprehension regarding the future. How long a 'future' would one have? On arriving at the station I became aware of other young men standing around looking very unsure of themselves. We had arrived, strangers thrown into the mixing-bowl together, and we stood around waiting.

A khaki-coloured lorry drew up outside and a short-haired Sergeant stepped out and walked across to us. "You men are the new recruits for this draft — follow me," he bellowed and we all climbed into the back of the lorry. That journey into camp was a strange experience; it was to be our last moments of freedom as civilians for quite a few years, and for me, nearly seven years before I was eventually demobbed.

We were fitted out with army uniforms and our civilian possessions were put away; this was the first levelling out procedure, all men had to be alike, hair was cut short, our battledress, forage caps, greatcoats, boots, socks and underwear, all exactly alike. We were each given a number and identity discs, and there we were, just a number in the 2nd Battalion of the Wiltshire

19

Regiment of Infantry, stationed in an old army barracks and facing a life of considerable hardship. We did not receive gentle treatment, we were shouted at, drilled in the square, forced to carry our packs on long route marches, climb hills at the double and then run backwards down again — not an easy exercise — and we learned to fight and endure together as a unit. At the end of the first six weeks we had been changed into men who could obey orders, and none of us were ever the same again.

We made friends and found a comaraderie that is hard to explain; we respected some and despised others. Our lives depended upon the reactions of the men we lived with in such close contact, twenty men to a hut, open washing facilities and a row of toilets for 100 men, with a tough Corporal and Sergeant in charge, living in a separate room at the end of our hut. They had sheets on their beds, we only had blankets. The obvious perks that the higher rank enjoyed gave a man the incentive to work his way out of the ranks.

I had one idea. I wanted promotion so I had a goal ahead of me, as I wanted to progress out of the life of a private and an ordinary soldier. It only took me a few months to become a Sergeant through taking several courses which, when passed, gave me promotion. I then had the comforts given to the higher ranks.

The first time I was promoted to Sergeant, I lost my head. I was over-confident and very cocksure, so without obtaining permission I walked out of camp one weekend and took the train home to tell my wife in person that I was now 'somebody', my three new stripes sewn on my arm.

When I was returning to camp, the train was stopped, redcaps boarded, and my name taken. I appeared before the CO, was demoted and reduced to the ranks, and transferred to another corps, the REME. I was once more back to square one, and with a posting to the Middle East! This was the way the army gave you another chance — they sent you into battle with another Regiment.

I had been fortunate because I had missed the BEF (British Expeditionary Force) that had served in France and been defeated. Our army had retreated back across the Channel from Dunkirk, and I had been on another course at the time.

This time I was to be sent to another battle front, I was to go to Egypt, but at the time I was not aware of the fact. I left Dover one night in 1940 by train, in the black-out. All the windows of the train were covered with black board and we could not see a thing. It was a long and uncomfortable journey, and after what seemed like eternity, we arrived and left the train, finding we were at Greenock in Scotland and about to embark into the unknown.

I must admit that I did not relish the idea of that sea voyage, and it has developed now into a phobia with me because I would never travel by boat again by choice. The journey was far worse than I had imagined.

We were marched in line down to the quayside and up the gangplank on to the ship. Someone called out to me: "Hurry up John"; my name was

'George', but from that time I was called 'John', and this name has stayed with me for the rest of my life. I was no longer 'George Pullen', I was 'John Pullen' — a different person.

We were marched down to the lower deck of the ship, and shut in. A hammock was given to each man which he slung on the beams. The men had to be so close together, their hammocks touched when the boat rolled. The deck was so low you had to keep your head down, and tall men found it very hard as they could not stand upright at all. I could just stand as I was only five feet six inches tall. We remain on this deck, feeding, washing, and trying to relax by playing cards, all in a very confined space, rarely seeing the light of day, and in this way we zigzagged across the Atlantic in convoy, avoiding German U-boats, and mines.

We heard sometimes that boats had been sunk, but we could not see what was going on above, and it was a terrifying experience to realize you were shut down below and really had very little chance of getting out, if anything had happened to the ship.

One of our stops was at Sierra Leone on the West Coast of Africa, and it was heaven to be able to go out into the sunshine and walk on terra firma again.

We stopped at Cape Town, and here the South African people welcomed us and took us into their homes. They were marvellous, and their hospitality was greatly appreciated by the troops.

Then to Port Said and our disembarkation. We landed in sight of the De Lesseps monument at the top of the Suez Canal, and we filed down the gangplanks on to the quay.

For a short while we lived under canvas in tents, training for desert warfare. I was attached to tank maintenance and I was made up to Sergeant once more. The battle for El Alemein was approaching, consequently my stay in the desert was remarkably short as I was soon blown up, and flown back wounded to South Africa with burns on my arms and legs.

Words cannot express how good the medical services were in the South African hospitals. I was encased in a special covering used for burns, and skin had to be grafted on to my feet and hands.

After six months I was ready again for action, and given a new position in the Catering Corps, when the most interesting part of my career commenced. I travelled extensively.

I sailed from Cape Town and landed after a short trip on Madagascar for a 'mopping up' period. We were only there a few days, and we rejoined the ship and sailed to India, landing at Bombay, walking through the famous gateway.

My next trip was to the north of India where I joined an American unit at Karachi, travelling through the country by train, a plain wooden construction with open windows and solid seats, in uncomfortable conditions. The American food was excellent, and when the train stopped, ice boxes were produced by the roadside, and we enjoyed the luxury of spam instead of the usual old bully beef and dried biscuits, and we had wonderful ice cold tea.

Whilst I was stationed at Karachi, I was detailed to go into Afghanistan and take supplies through the Khyber Pass. The scenery was magnificent, with indescribable sunsets; my memories here are of the great beauty of the countryside. I enjoyed the travelling.

My duties finished in India and I was sent to Basra, a desert station in Iraq and very hot, the temperature being 120° at midnight, and we all suffered from prickly heat, an uncomfortable rash. Sometimes we could have a break and go by train to the YMCA hostel at Baghdad for a week's leave, which was a welcome break.

I travelled a great deal whilst I was stationed at Basra. I made a trip to Beirut, and across the desert to Jerusalem and Damascus, and I saw many beautiful highly decorated mosques and buildings in the particularly delightful Indian architecture.

Kuwait, on the Persian Gulf, was a small town comprised of mud and timber-framed houses with flat roofs, so entirely different from the modern buildings of today, which I recently noted on television. No doubt if I returned again to any of the countries I travelled through, I should find it impossible to recognize any of it. Over the years so much has changed — the past is over — I returned to England when I was demobbed, no longer a boy, but a hard, seasoned man.

My Own Experiences

by George Evans Holley

When war was declared with Germany in September 1939 it was widely expected that war planes might attack London at any time. Plans were therefore hastily made to evacuate schoolchildren to safer areas, and students like myself, then training as teachers at Goldsmiths' College, as courses were temporarily suspended, mostly offered to accompany schools as auxiliary teachers, to help establish children in accommodation which was being arranged for them.

In this capacity I was asked to report to the Headmaster at Peckham Park School on a day when all pupils and available staff were preparing to leave and say tearful goodbyes to their parents. Each member of the party, apart from personal belongings, carried a box about nine inches cubed containing the inevitable gas mask. Nobody knew at the time of leaving where we were making for, but the first objective was Denmark Hill Station. Then a train appeared with scores of other children already aboard and in almost holiday mood we were on our way to a mystery destination.

It soon became apparent that we were heading in the direction of Brighton. The south coast seemed a strange objective but even more surprising was the ultimate destination of our party, Shoreham-by-Sea, a busy little port with industries near by which to me seemed quite as vulnerable as the outskirts of London. The ways the official mind works are however seldom explicable by rational standards.

Only a few days later, after arriving at Shoreham, I received notification that Goldsmiths' students were to report to Nottingham University where facilities were available for us to attend lectures partly with our own and partly with Nottingham staff.

Founded by Jesse Boot at Beeston, where also are situated the dispensing laboratories and experimental laboratories of the Boots manufacturing retail chemists, the University buildings and grounds were impressive in their grandeur and I was pleased to take part in the sports facilities provided, as vice-captain of the college cricket team and member of the rowing club which operated on the River Trent. I was allocated lodgings in the town in Wilford Grove, very near to Trent Bridge cricket and football grounds and overshadowed by the hill on which stands Nottingham Castle and at the base

23

of which is a famous public house, The Trip to Jerusalem.

Conditions for study in the University were excellent and here I was able to spend a memorable year completing my BA Degree and Teachers Training Course. The successful completion of the three years' course meant that I would be qualified to take up teaching immediately after the war and I was promised a post in the London area provided I was still medically fit.

My one year postponement of military service having expired, as I was of military age at the outset and I would no doubt have been involved in the British Expeditionary Force in France where many of my friends were either wounded, captured or killed, I reported to the 55th Royal Tank Regiment, Royal Armoured Corps at Farnborough, Hants.

Initial square bashing which I shared with Richard Greene the actor later well known as Robin Hood and the star of many other films, was followed by training in tank warfare. This consisted of gunnery relating to the use of and firing of rifles, revolvers, Besa and Bren machine-guns and two-pounder tank and anti-tank guns and mechanical engineering relating to the handling of tracked vehicles such as Bren-gun carriers, leading on to the Cruiser tank with twin-banked eight-cylinder Rolls-Royce engines.

Naturally, tracked-vehicle driving instruction was the pleasantest feature at this stage when first with Bren-carriers and later with light and medium tanks we went out each day in groups with friendly instructors. Thus we got to know all the surrounding countryside in the vicinity of Frensham Common, Hindhead, Farnham and the Hog's Back — even driving a Cruiser tank up Guildford High Street — and we discovered the location of many cafés and refreshment stalls where we could get tea and cakes, which the old-soldier NCOs called 'char' and 'wads'.

When I qualified as Tank Driver-Mechanic, I was drafted to the Queen's Bays Armoured Cavalry Regiment then stationed at Milford cross-roads near Godalming, Surrey with the 10th Hussars (Shiny Tenth) and 9th Royal Lancers. They formed the 22nd Armoured Brigade of the 1st Armoured Division — three regiments which according to their names and traditions should have been equipped wth horses rather than mechanical beasts, for they were classed as mechanized cavalry.

With me from Farnborough came a character named Ernie Trory, an avowed Communist and unashamed scrounger who had brought the practice of getting out of duties to a fine art. A doctor's certificate (probably forged) testified that he had flat feet. This piece of paper got him out of many parades until the Sergeant-Major, old 'chota' John as we called him, asked to see it and ceremoniously tore it up in small shreds.

As we had been drafted into 3 Troop 'B' Squadron at the same time the regulars of all ranks tended from the beginning to bracket us together as if I was responsible for Ernie, but I did not take his attitude too seriously and was always prepared to see the funny side of his antics and mimes and share his jokes. In our free time we managed some pleasant jaunts and hikes in the countryside around the area and sized up the local talent at Elstead and Godalming. We joined in the Saturday 'hops' when possible. Ernie always slouched along with his carefully assumed flat-foot gait.

At meal times Ernie always used his own knife, fork and spoon marked 'Trory's Café Brighton'. After the war I was amazed to see in a newspaper in mid-winter, a picture of a group of frozen looking bathers with Ernie unmistakably in the middle of the group. It bore the caption 'Ernie and his friends never miss their early-morning dip'. The flat feet must have been as effective as frogmen's flippers.

This phase of my army career was too good to last. Ernie Trory was suddenly withdrawn from the regiment and sent back to Brigade Head-quarters where afterwards we heard his background was investigated, but doubtless he had achieved his own objective and 'worked his ticket'. Later we heard that he was discharged with ignominy.

It now became clear that our equipment was being brought up to strength for direct participation in the battles being waged and planned abroad. Soon we were on stand-by and ready to move with all leave cancelled. On October 15th we left Milford as a Brigade and drove tanks and other vehicles to transporters waiting in sidings near Guildford Station. Then we were away northwards on a journey which took us to Greenock on the River Clyde and aboard a scruffy looking troop transport ship named undeservedly *Empire Pride*, part of a huge convoy being assembled in the river mouth. No time was wasted as we were potential sitting ducks for bombers, and the same night we slid away from our moorings. Soon we were out of the Firth of Clyde and moving south-west past Ireland and the Bay of Biscay.

Off the coast of Africa we enjoyed seeing and were fascinated by schools of porpoises and large numbers of flying fish following the ship. The porpoises bobbed in and out of the water like swimmers doing the butterfly crawl and the flying fish broke the surf, took a few frantic flaps of the wings and returned below the surface as they seemed to try to keep up with the ship. After a few days we were again in sight of land and called in at Freetown, Sierra Leone for refuelling. We dropped anchor in the mouth of the Rokel river and the idea that this was Africa made the land on either side seem very mysterious although it was not particularly distinguished for its beauty. Unfortunately there was no access to the shore and natives came swimming out with bananas which we were all under strict orders not to buy. Perhaps they could have been contaminated or injected with poison.

However we were greatly amused by the antics of some of the natives who dived and swam magnificently, especially when they were encouraged with 'Glasgow Tanners'.

Then we moved into the next stage of our journey, crossing the Equator with all the traditional ceremony of visiting the domains of King Neptune and speculation was growing as to our next port of call — would it be Cape Town or Durban? As it happened the convoy separated into two — we who were for the Middle East went into Cape Town while the others who were for the Far East went on to Durban to face the rapidly advancing Japanese.

As the ships of the convoy steamed into Table Bay with mighty Table Mountain looming up behind, the war seemed very remote and it was like a return to peacetime conditions. Wonderfully enthusiastic and patriotic white South African families turned up with their cars to welcome us and offered trips to delightful beaches along the coast. Along with a fellow tank crew member, wireless operator John Turner, I went to a beach resort called Muizenberg where we were able to enjoy the sea air of the Indian Ocean. This was far better than staying in Cape Town, a large part of which was out of bounds. Unfortunately the break came to an end all too soon and we continued our journey northwards after four days.

A few more days passed and we came by the Gulf of Aden to the Red Sea and by the Gulf of Suez to Port Tufiq where we entrained for Alexandria. This was a remarkable journey which brought us close to the Suez Canal and the River Nile, but in the crowded railway carriages it was difficult to appreciate the remarkable landscape of half-flooded fields where farmers were cultivating their crops. Their methods appeared very old-fashioned yet effective and the oxen working and yoked together presented a fascinating sight.

The final stage of the journey was by lorry and truck transport to a large transit camp area where we were shortly to take over our regimental armoured and transport vehicles. As we looked back over the past two months, the journey seemed to have been a remarkable experience and sleeping in a hammock one of the unforgettable ones.

During the next three weeks we got used to handling and driving the tanks on sandy surfaces and under desert warfare conditions. There were general tactical exercises and even mock battles. The tanks needed plenty of running in and the crews had to get used to procedures and working together. By a strange coincidence at this time I made the acquaintance of a member of the squadron which my 3 Troop was a part. He lived in Sydenham — very close to myself. His name was Ted Richmond and he very shortly found a legitimate way of getting out of the firing line. He had a very valuable inventive ability and designed a stove which could be adapted for use by tank crews on the move and which could be made with available materials such as cans and other food containers. He was withdrawn from his tank crew and employed in the Brigade Headquarters.

All this time the First Armoured Division of which we formed the Twenty-Second Armoured Brigade, was being brought up to strength by the arrival in the Alexandria area of units of the Royal Horse Artillery (mechanized of course), units of the Fourth Indian Division and a South African Armoured Brigade. Some on a rota basis had managed a few days' leave in Cairo but all was cancelled when it became known that a move towards the action was imminent.

The German and Italian troops of the Axis Army under Rommel had established a line beyond Tobruk between El Gazala and Bir Hacheim behind an extensive minefield and our objective would be to smash this line and relieve Tobruk, which was itself beseiged. It was known also that small groups of forces of Rommel's Afrika Korps were operating on a hit and run basis using their 88 millimetre guns with devastating effect.

In early April 1942 we moved off in battle formation but well spaced out. Our progress continued unhampered for several days and we passed Mersa Matruh where there was a large field hospital, and Sidi Barrani. After Sollum we passed through Hell-Fire Pass as Wadi Haifa was known, and the signs of many battles were all too obvious. The wrecks of German, Italian and British armoured vehicles of all kinds littered the desert. These we often half-buried in the sand with other more gruesome relics such as smashed in helmets, boots and clothing. Jerrycans abounded but we kept clear of them as they were likely to be booby-trapped. The Italians had been put to flight in this area in 1941 at Msus and the occasion was commemorated as the 'Msus Stakes' when all previous records of the speed of retreat had been broken.

We were in Cyrenaica now, part of Libya, and came upon a great battle area near Sidi Razegh where Rommel's forces had severly mauled a British force.

Although the heat was stifling in the daytime, the nights were very cold and we slept on groundsheets which had been placed against tank tracks on the leeward side. Unfortunately these seemed to attract unwelcome insect visitors like white scorpions, and I remember waking when it was light enough to see a large specimen very close to my right ear and ready to strike.

Frequently on the horizon in the shimmering heat, enemy vehicles appeared and it was difficult to determine whether they were real or illusory in the conditions. All the time groups of Arabs were wandering about the desert, and as it was known that they were in the habit of giving information about our whereabouts and numbers to the enemy, they had to be driven away and sometimes mown down by machine-gun fire.

More and more often now enemy reconnaissance planes appeared high in the sky and we witnessed many dog-fights between these and our own protective fighter planes. Then on the 16th May in the morning the unmistakable sound of a Stuka dive-bomber screaming down and bang! bang! bang! followed by the rattle of machine-gun fire, made it clear that we were under attack. Escorting anti-aircraft guns were quickly manned and the next Stuka to appear got a hot reception. Sticks of bombs landed harmlessly between the tanks of our squadron and we were able to continue our advance without damage or casualties, but the experience of the Stukas diving out of the sun as if they would land right on us before they flattened out to pass overhead, was one we would never forget

Towards the end of May we were on the outskirts of Tobruk and our task was to bypass that port and break the Axis line at the Gazola end near the sea.

We were supported by a splendid force of Ghurka troops of the Fourth India Division and the Fifth South African Brigade of armoured cars and scout cars from Natal.

Suddenly it became apparent that the leading tanks of our Regimental Commander Colonel Draffen and the second in command Viscount Lord Knebworth had run into trouble and were being attacked as they reached the edge of a minefield. They and their tanks were blown to bits by the 88 millimetre guns mounted on the Tiger Tanks of the Afrika Korps. These were far more powerful then the 'pea-shooter' two-pounder guns on our tanks and Captain Lyle led our troop to temporary respite after directing some fire against some enemy transport vehicles.

On the 3rd June our somewhat depleted regiment joined in with other armoured units of the Brigade to penetrate the enemy defensive line. A clear way through the minefield seemed to have been found for an advance in strength. Suddenly however, we were proved wrong. There was an explosion on the left side and the track was severed by the front sprocket. Paddy Rattigan, the wireless operator, notified the engineers of the support group of our position, and a truck came to pick us up to find the regimental headquarters. However the enemy were already counter-attacking and we came under fire. The driver was killed by a direct hit and I dived out the other side and took refuge in a depression in the rocky ground. As the lorry 'brewed up' I realized that I had sustained some shrapnel injuries and others, who had been in the vehicle beside the gunner and tank commander Sergeant Rumsey, had taken separate shelter. Although I only seemed to have flesh wounds, some blood was flowing from my arm, leg and head. Suddenly a scout car appeared at the head of a group of vehicles. The high rocky cliffs had obscured their approach. I was immediately confronted by a smart officer holding a revolver, who I was amazed to realize was Italian. There was clearly no way of escape. Other soldiers quickly appeared at his side and I was offered immediate first aid treatment.

In the circumstances I felt entirely in agreement with Falstaff in Shakespeare's *Henry IV* Part 1, when he says: "The better part of valour is discretion." I was relieved to be cleaned up and bandaged. This degree of attention must have made me look even more of a casualty than I really was, for from then on I was treated very correctly and sympathetically. I was able to talk to them in French and I found out that this Italian Force was part of the famous Ariete (Arrow) Division, probably the best Italian troops. I was assured that I would be taken in a hospital ship, rather than linger with the ever growing number of Eighth Army prisoners being herded together with little immediate prospect of getting out of the scorching desert sun.

Three days later I was on board a hospital ship crossing the Mediterranean and the following night we were in the Bay of Naples, a far distance from the Bay of Cape Town which had been so brightly illuminated, although subdued compared with peacetime. We were not there for sightseeing however, and soon we were in large lorries climbing into the volcanic region of the Apennines.

The destination turned out to be Benevento, the scene of a great battle between the Romans and Carthaginians in early times (246 BC). Here I had my first experience of being inside a barbed wire compound, with the familiar looking watch towers at each corner from which searchlights swept periodically over the camp all night, keeping the perimeters under observation. Accommodation took the form of large tents sheltering about twenty men in each. We were provided with straw mattresses and there were four ablution and toilet blocks of wooden construction. Time passed slowly here as there were no facilities for useful activities.

However, after about three weeks we were on our way to a more permanent camp and I arrived about the end of July at PG 52, further into the hills at Caserta. Here we enjoyed the comparative luxury of wooden barrack type huts and a large recreation and dining hall. Sports equipment had been supplied by the Red Cross so that football, cricket and table tennis could be played outside, and in the recreation hall was a stage where we saw the possibility of organizing entertainments, such as concerts and plays. Among the 240 assembled here were several talented actors, singers and musicians, and in a short time plans were afoot for a spectacular production of the *Mikado*. The score of the operetta was obtained and many worked hard making scenery, stage properties and clothes for the players. Others got to work with paint to make a background. Those who were brave enough to take on female parts came in for some good-natured ribbing, particularly from the old soldiers. Even musical instruments were obtained from the Red Cross.

As autumn approached, some who had specialist knowledge arranged to pass it on to groups interested and a kind of Adult Education Institute was organized. I got together a group who were interested in learning or improving their French and apart from conversation we arranged some sketches and short plays.

Thus with reasonable Italian food available which could sometimes be rendered more palatable with the contents of Red Cross parcels, life at this stage seemed quite tolerable. The Italians took little notice except to check numbers fairly regularly. Yet even then there were signs that the situation would change in short time. German columns were constantly moving southwards, for British troops who had turned the tables on the Axis armies at El Alamein were already in Sicily.

One night however, I was struck by excrutiating pains in the stomach and knew very little more until I woke up to find myself in a spotlessly clean modern hospital. Nursing Nuns whom we called Sorella (Sister) were walking about in white attire and the contrast with being in a rough prisoner of war camp seemed overwhelming at first. I got the impression that I was in another world and for some unaccountable reason had qualified for admittance to the more comfortable of the two. The situation of the hospital was Chiavari, a mountainous forested region south-east of Genoa.

During the next few weeks life was very pleasant as I was convalescing, and the view from the top floor of this hospital which was reserved for war prisoners was delightful. In the same ward as myself were some badly wounded white South African soldiers who were wonderfully cheerful and friendly. I can remember them singing Afrikaan songs like Zucker Boss (Sugar Bush) and Saree Marais. Considering the magnificent contribution these men and thousands of others made to our war effort, it is disgusting to hear their country being insulted and sportsmen being punished for wanting to take part in competitive sports with them.

I learned a lot of Italian with the help of the nurses in that hospital and was striving hard to become as fluent as possible, knowing that it would be very important to be able to use the language if I got free, as I intended to when fully fit, as the Swiss and French borders seemed invitingly near.

However about this time — early summer 1943, the Allied Anglo-American forces got control of Sicily and were preparing to invade Italy, when the Germans moved in to transfer all prisoners of war to Germany. At this time many made desperate bids for freedom, but in my convalescent state it was impossible to profit from the chaotic situation which enabled some to reach Switzerland, though I was able to help some to get on their way by finding out ways of getting clear of the hospital.

Soon I found myself on a train which was on its way through Austria and Hungary into Silesia, a part of Poland which the Germans had already annexed. All place names had been made German sounding, thus Kattowice became Kattowitz.

The landscape was now very different. Instead of the beautiful beforested region of the Apennines, the grey countryside was scattered with coal-mine shafts. We arrived at Oehringen between Gleiwitz and Kattowitz — it was clear that we were expected to work at the mines — above ground, *Ubertage*, or underground, *Untertage*, according to physical fitness. I avoided underground owing to my recent operation. The stamm lager (concentration camp or POW camp) or Stalag 8B was situated between two mines (Gruben), Ostfeld (East Field) and Westfeld (Westfield) and was again the typical looking POW camp such as one has since seen of Auschwitz (which was situated quite near). There were watch towers in the four corners, from which searchlights swung round at night on double rows of stacheldraht (spiky barbed wire) with rolls of barbed wire in between allegedly electrified. Owing to the proximity of coal we were not short of hot water for washing and showers, and fuel for the iron boilers in the huts on which we could find corners for brewing drinks.

The guards were members of the Volksturm (German equivalent of Home Guard) often recruited locally or too old or pensioned off from military service. Each day groups of us prisoners marched off to the Ostfeld or Westfeld mines with a guard front and rear and were put in the charge of a 'steiger' or foreman who wanted some task performed, like loading or unloading a truck of bricks or iron girders. I, as spokesman, usually established that it was *Akkord Arbeit* and if the reply was *Ferrig dann Feierabend*, it meant that when the job was done we would be finished for the day and could go back to camp.

As time went on we got to know our way around the mine and who was to be found in the various little sheds or *Buden*. Some were friendly Ukranians or Poles with whom we could carry out *Geschaft* (business) such as exchanging cigarettes from Red Cross parcels for pamphlets dropped by the RAF or American Flying Fortress bombers, which supplied useful information about the state of the war, and were illustrated with sketch maps. It was amazing what could be obtained by exchanging the contents of Red Cross parcels! Some of us built up quite a stock of minute bottles of drinks, but we had to find some ingenious hideaways for them when the Jerries came round on their occasional searches. As we passed through the village on the way to the mine or under special escort to the dentists we were amused by posters on which appeared slogans like *Rader Mussen Rollen fue der Sieg* (Wheels must turn for Victory) or *PSST! Feind hort Mit* (Shush! the enemy is listening). Back home we had the slogan 'Careless Talk costs lives', but the Poles used to sing a pleasant little song which went:

> *Es geht alles voruber*
> *Es geht alles vorbei*
> *Zuerst geht der Fuhrer*
> *Dann geht die Partei.*

meaning

All will soon be over
and done with — first
goes the leader (Hitler)
then the Nazi Party.

One interesting character we called 'Blinker' who had been badly shell-shocked. He was often foreman on building operations but took his nickname in good part. He was always ready to trade in various food items for cigarettes which were ideal currency. The more cigarettes we could get, the more trading we could do, so our health benefited because the 'fags' were too good to smoke! The Ukranian girls in the stores were very friendly when we gave them cigarettes and we had quite a party when they brought along some Schnapps.

Thus the time went along fairly quickly until autumn 1944 when we realized that the Germans were getting 'edgy' because the Russians were breaking through in the east and Allied forces were making progress in the west. By January 1945 it became apparent that we should soon be moving out. Rumours had it that the Russian forward tanks were already on the outskirts of Cracow and could overtake us before we got very far.

At about 7 p.m. on Monday 22nd January 1944 on a dark night snow was falling steadily and the ground was very slippery. The Germans started blowing whistles and came round telling everyone to pick up their belongings and get outside the huts. *RAUS! RAUS!* was the call, and there was such a commotion I can hear it now. Shortly afterwards after the inevitable roll-call, we all marched out of Stalag 8B for the last time. We staggered along through the night and I realized that we were moving in the direction of Ratibor where we would cross the river Oder.

It was difficult to imagine what might lie ahead as our column moved slowly along. Luckily most of us had some food in our overcoat pockets. Nothing was provided or available for us in the first twenty-four hours, but that evening we came to a Malt Factory at Great Peterwitz and were thankful to be able to partake of potato and swede soup boiled up in a rusty old vat. Here some of us were able to knock together pieces of wood to devise makeshift sledges and got hold of rope or string so as to pull along our belongings. Then we contrived to rest and get some sleep on the factory floor.

The weather was bitterly cold and many of us were wondering how long we would be able to struggle along like this. For the next four or five weeks there was no let up in conditions that would normally seem intolerable. Snow remained piled up at roadsides and over fields and the atmosphere was foggy as well as frozen. The very conditions seemed like a prison but there seemed very little object in breaking out of it. There seemed to be a kind of safety in numbers and the ironic fact was that our so-called guards were apparently more miserable than we were. We at least, had the prospect of moving towards our own Allies although we felt a little dubious as to what it would be like if the Russkies found us first.

At least we put on a show of cheerfulness, enjoying our own private jokes at the expense of the Volksturm, singing songs and using army language and expressions they knew could not be very complimentary. It was a good job they were not SS troops whom we sometimes saw in charge of groups of political prisoners and Jews whom they treated cruelly and more like animals.

On the night of 28th January we stopped for the night at Leobschutz and crossed next day into the Sudetenland near Jagerndorf. Food was very scarce all the time and sometimes when we stopped at farmhouses we took anything we could find, either to eat on the spot or to make into soup later on. Sometimes we unearthed potatoes and swedes from where they had been stored and made our own soups when possible.

By the 1st February we were making for Chemnitz, an important industrial centre, and progressed via Zwittan and Krokendorf towards Alstadt which we reached by 8th February. On the 12th we passed into the Bohemias protectorate and spent a night in another brick factory at Osik.

There was a noticeable air of friendliness among people who came out of the houses to greet us. The Volksturm seemed disinterested and did not object when some villagers brought us out hot coffee and new rye bread at Oberjellan. The following day we were on the outskirts of Konigsgratz.

On 2nd March we crossed the river Elbe by the Stephan Bridge at Melnick which is situated only 28 kilometres from Prague, and we all cheered when Flying Fortresses flew over, coming from the direction of Dresden to the north-west of us at that time.

The country was now very wooded as we continued in the direction of Karlsbad and towards the mountainous region of the Erzgebirge. When we arrived at Marienbad we came upon a storage depot for Red Cross supplies. It had recently been abandoned, and much taken, apparently by the local population. We could hardly believe our eyes but naturally took what we could, especially cigarettes which would again stand us in good stead as currency. Unfortunately the rich food was too much for stomachs accustomed to raw potatoes, swedes and stale bread.

As the days became longer and the weather more spring like, the country became very beautiful, but by now many of us were feeling distinctly weak. It seemed almost as if we were slogging on through a dream world of pine forests. We were now near the Bavarian border and it was not entirely imagination which caused us to hear the occasional sound of distant gunfire. The question was — were we hearing the Russians behind or the Americans ahead — or both?

At this stage the column we had been marching with began to break up into small groups. The Volksturm guards were thinking more of their own safety than of keeping their eyes on us. Yet we felt ironically enough that it would be better to stay in the vicinity of the guards where we would be less likely to be attacked by fleeing SS, who in their desperation might be trigger-happy and ready to use up a few bullets on escapees.

By the 27th March we were 8 kilometres from Weiden at Floss on the river Naab. Here we found a large barn which offered shelter. The farmer offered us food it we did a few odd jobs around the farm. Bill Woolley and I spent some time stacking snow shields, a form of fencing erected during winter storms as protection of poultry and rabbit pens against driving snow. Then a lorry load of German soldiers came along. They had got hold of some Red Cross parcels and offered to take us into Weiden where there were hot showers and a clothing cleansing unit where some fresh clothing might be available. We availed ourselves of the opportunity and felt quite fresh and smart afterwards.

On the 14th April at 7 a.m. a German infantry unit (559 Company) which had been rounding up groups of prisoners wandering about in the area, distributed some more Red Cross parcels and got us all organized, advising us not to resort to any more looting at this stage, as there was little object in risking getting shot.

A new and more organized march began into Southern Germany in the direction of Straubing. We crossed the Danube at 1.30 a.m. as the German plan was apparently to move us around at night while staying quiet during the daytime.

Then on 1st May on the outskirts of Amfing, it became apparent that the guards themselves had become more and more perturbed by some news they had received and it was rumoured that an American tank force had been reported not far away. The group of about thirty of us decided that if the guards became less vigilant and more inclined to look after themselves, we would break up into groups of two or three. That night Woolley and I decided to try our luck and get away. All we knew was that we were in the area between the rivers Inn and Danube, and Munich was not far away.

Rather than go into Amfing we decided to look for a small village. At a cottage on the outskirts of Weilskirchen an elderly couple said we could take shelter in the hay loft of a small barn and they brought us some food. In fact we remained there for two more nights and only came out when the light was bad. The comparatively restful time was spoiled for me however, as stomach trouble and sickness seemed to have overtaken me just at a time when I wanted to be really fit. Clearly the availability of some good food posed problems for my run-down digestive system.

As American troops got nearer they were driving before them Nazi agents who knew that anyone they came across might be a threat and Herr Meyer who had been protecting us was getting more and more jittery. We could not help feeling that, although we felt very grateful to him, he might be forced to disclose our presence and it was hardly fair to put him in this position.

When a stranger appeared in the lane who seemed a possible Nazi we decided to get out hurriedly by the back door, thanking the couple for their hospitality. We ran along a hedge and got into a wooded area. Then by following footpaths we came on to a country road. Hearing the sound of an approaching vehicle we listened carefully and heard the familiar sound of a tracked vehicle — like chains being dragged along the ground and making a screeching noise on the hard surface.

The big question was, whose tanks? There were three possibilities, German, Russian or American. It was almost an anticlimax when we realized it was an old, battle-scarred Sherman tank lumbering along, and that the crew were unmistakably Americans. We had heard bad reports about the performance of Sherman tanks in the desert, but this was for us a very good Sherman, an up-dated model with a powerful looking gun.

The crew told us to hop up quick, without time for ceremonial greetings, as they had been scouting around from Landshut where they had established a temporary base. When we got to the village we found a reception centre had been set up. We were soon fixed up with a shower and some fresh clothing and a doctor came round to examine us. It didn't take long for the doctor to decide that like many others I had yellow jaundice and was a priority case for repatriation.

It was 8th May and I said goodbye to Woolley, when a lorry came along to take a group of us to Regensburg where we had further medical check-ups. The next day I could hardly believe it when I heard that I would be on the next Dakota flight to 'somewhere in England'. That somewhere turned out to be Banbury, Oxfordshire, but it was decided I was not yet ready to go back to London. My spirits were high but my physical condition was apparently worse than I felt. It was decided that I should spend a short while convalescing in Wakefield Hospital and getting treatment for the condition brought on by malnutrition and a liver infection. It was 18th May before I was finally able to go home.

Two weeks later I reported to Bury St. Edmunds to go through the procedures of demobilization and be fitted for my 'demob suit'!

Wartime Recollections

by Edna Lucy Antrobus

Not until I contemplated writing these recollections, did I realize what a wild, uncharted stretch of life I had to disentangle from the fading years. Against a background of bombs and black-out and evacuation, my own circumstances with their hopes and emotions and insecurity drove me in disorderly progression to no safe conclusion.

When the war broke out we were living in Beckenham, Kent; my husband Harvey, was working at 'The Wellcome Foundation', Langley Court, within a few minutes of our house, and we had a little girl, Celia Rosemary, known as 'Wookey', who was about three and a half. People, especially those with children, were thinking of going away if they could. My mother's sister, with whom my mother was living at that time, had a beautiful old house near Totnes in Devonshire which had secret passages down to the river Dart. My aunt and cousins and my mother went to stay there during July 1939, and Wookey and I joined them a little later. Unfortunately they could not live in the house as my aunt had let it some time before, so they had to live in caravans in the orchard and my mother and Wookey and I went to stay in a nearby farm. The countryside looked lovely in the sunshine of the late summer and I enjoyed picking up apples and helping with the harvest, but any beauty that the farm had was an illusion. It was unkempt and dirty and hens and other animals roamed in and around the kitchen. The wife spent all her time by the range and the farmer spent all his time in the local pub; his elder son did most of the work. I was glad to be able to escape to a nearby paper mill where I worked for some weeks, riding a bicycle to and fro. When at last we heard Neville Chamberlain on the radio telling us that war was declared, I was kneeling in the hall trying to paint an ancient push-chair that we wanted to use for Wookey. I was humming 'On the Sunny Side of the Street' which seems in restrospect to have been rather inappropriate.

Some weeks passed and nothing alarming happened, so my aunt decided to pack up her family and the mountains of tins of food she had brought in case we starved, and to return home. My mother too, could not go back fast enough, but I stayed on with Wookey for a short while. However, although everyone was very fond of 'the little maid', I was not so welcome, and when the farmer's wife accused me of stealing a diamond ring that my mother had

36

given her, I knew it was time to leave.

During the autumn of 1939 we experienced what became known as the 'phoney war'. My aunt had taken her younger children to South Africa by this time, so my mother came to stay with us. Most people became lulled into a sense of false security at that time. I certainly did; I was not nervous of possible danger, but on the other hand I did not want to discuss bombs or war or the uncertain future. My amateur drama activities had ceased with the war, but I buried my head in my own affairs and read and saw my friends and went out when I could. Wookey was a very bright little girl and we knew that she was ready for school when she was four, so in April 1940 we sent her to Dartrey House School, which was only a short distance along the road; she was four years and three months.

So life continued much as usual until the bombs at last began to fall and we found ourselves facing the reality of war which we called the Battle of Britain. We had had black-out frames made for all our windows, and the hall shored up with wooden pillars from floor to ceiling. Harvey had made an eight foot high semicircle of sandbags outside the front door. We had a large cupboard under the stairs and Wookey thought it was fun to sleep in there with my mother. By this time I was expecting a baby and I slept on a mattress near the front door. Sirens were sounding regularly almost every night and we lost all our windows more than once. One house opposite us had been cut in two, with one half completely demolished, and many others near by had been badly damaged. My mother slept very little and Harvey roamed around most of the night; but I slept, and when a bomb fell I jumped six inches, said "Another bomb?" and turned over and went to sleep again. Everyone in the south-east corner of England knew by now that they were living in 'Bomb Alley'; when enemy aircraft from the Continent had been on a London raid, they dropped any surplus bombs on their way back to the coast, or they mistook us for Biggin Hill and raided us anyway.

Harvey was getting very uneasy about our still being there, and one day he came home from Langley Court much later than usual as he had been waiting for a raid to end. He said he was taking us away next morning. When we asked where we were going he said that Cirencester was the only place he had heard about that wasn't already teeming with evacuees, both official and unofficial. We threw some clothes into cases and I had to take another one filled with clothes and little necessaries for the baby. I don't remember anything about the actual journey except that the train was crowded, but I know that we arrived quite late at night and without any luggage; we realized that this must have been left behind on the platform at Paddington Station. We walked the streets looking for some kind of lodging, if only for the night, but with no luck, and the number of people who were also wandering about seemed to belie the rumour that this Gloucestershire town was still unaware of the London exodus. Finally in desperation Harvey led us to the police station. When the police learned that we had nowhere to go, they said we had been very unwise to have come, but they offered to take us to a lodging for just the one night. We walked through the now quieter streets and came to a tall old dark house which would have seemed sinister in more normal circumstances. We were taken down into the basement to a big old-fashioned kitchen and were given a meal, there were just a man and a woman there.

We were very hungry and tired and after we had eaten I was told that my room with Wookey was on the third floor. I can picture the little four-year-old stepping out happily and trustfully in front of me up all those steep and bare old stairs. The bedroom was large and the bed was large and very comfortable. I asked Wookey if I should stay with her but she said: "No Mummy, I'm very sleepy," and indeed she was asleep before I left the room. I don't know where my mother slept but Harvey stayed in the basement on an old sofa. I never saw anyone else in the house. Next morning after breakfast we went back to the police station as arranged and they asked Harvey why he had come to Cirencester in particular and whether he had any friends in the neighbourhood. Reluctantly Harvey admitted that he had a brother near Gloucester.

"Well then . . . " they said.

"No," said Harvey, "we only write a short note at Christmas and I haven't seen him for over twenty years."

That seemed no obstacle to the police, and though Harvey warned them that Ernest would not be on the phone, they smiled and carried on with their enquiries. Finally they came and told us that his nearest neighbour lived at Stone End Farm about half a mile up the road, and that the farmer had sent someone to fetch Ernest. A typically Antrobus conversation took place between the brothers.

Ernest: "That you Harvey?"
Harvey: "Yes, we're stuck in Cirencester."
Ernest: "What's the trouble?"
Harvey: "I've brought the family away."
Ernest: "Get a bit rough?"
Harvey: "Yes, they want somewhere to stay."
Ernest: "You'd better come here. Get the next train to Gloucester."
Harvey: "Taxi?"
Ernest: "No, I'll meet you."

And so he did, in a battered old Austin, and that was how we arrived at The Bungalow, Churcham, four miles from Gloucester. Hilda came down the path to welcome us as if we were their nearest and dearest. Neither of them knew that Harvey had been divorced and had married me six years before. They showed no surprise when they saw me — and Wookey — and my mother. We owed them a great deal.

The bungalow had been built fairly recently but had no modern conveniences, i.e. no electricity, no gas, no water, and moreover, no bathroom and no inside WC. Hilda did the cooking on a small range in the living-room and on a Primus stove. There was a kitchen, living-room and two bedrooms. Their two sons who were still at school, slept in the smaller room. Ernest had moved out some time before into an Anderson shelter that he had had built just outside the back door, and Hilda, who had slept in solitary state in the larger bedroom, moved out to sleep on the sofa so that we could have her room. Privately mother and I were rather amused at the luxury of the Anderson shelter, and on another occasion soon after we arrived, Hilda said gravely: "I don't know why you came here, we have bombs too you know. One dropped in Mr Corry's field recently." When asked where that was, she pointed to a hill about a mile away. We forbore to tell them too much too soon and only gradually made them understand the conditions in Beckenham and the south of London. Luckily when Harvey went back to Paddington after delivering us, he was able to trace our lost luggage which we received in due course.

We had, of course, to cancel my booking at the Stone Park Maternity Home, Beckenham, and as the baby was due in a month's time, I had to do something about booking up in Gloucester. There were only about three buses a day to town and, my goodness, you had to stand in the road and wave both arms if you wanted to stop them in their mad career, and even then they often blinked a blind eye. However, I did manage to get to Gloucester soon after we arrived. Hilda had told me that there was only one Maternity Home, and she should know I thought, having lived there for about twenty years. So I followed her directions and arrived at the home which was in Barton Street. I was shown in to see the Matron and after talking amicably for a while, she asked me when the baby was due. When I said 29th October, she was shocked.

"Good gracious," she said, "we have no vacancies before March!" As I was leaving rather hurriedly, a friendly nurse advised me to go to see the Medical Officer of Health. So slightly daunted I made my way to the Shire Hall in Westgate. The lady MOH was very charming to me. She said that more and more official evacuee mothers-to-be were arriving in Gloucestershire, and that a Maternity Home was being opened in a college for ladies in Cheltenham, which had been taken over for that purpose. I would be welcome to go there, she said. In retrospect this lady doctor was amazingly like Joyce Grenfell in one of her character sketches, she even looked like her. "They've called it 'Sunnyside Maternity Home', *isn't* that a lovely name?" she asked, and she wriggled coyly and beamed her reassurance. As it was about twelve miles from Churcham to Cheltenham, she warned me that I must go there three days before the baby was due.

Wookey went to the village school in the Church Hall and she loved it. We made ourselves comfortable at the bungalow but we knew that we must try to find somewhere else to stay after the baby arrived; we could not go on inconveniencing Ernest and his family indefinitely.

On 26th October I packed my bag and Ernest and I rattled our way to

Cheltenham, where he said goodbye to me downstairs in the ante-natal ward. Here I met the 'official' evacuees. They came from Ipswich and from London's East End. I was a lone wolf among two strange packs and I couldn't understand what any of them were saying. The unfamiliar Suffolk dialect was naturally difficult, but I had never realized how unintelligible real cockney could be. I soon understood that I was being ostracized, and this had nothing to do with the language problem. A nurse told me the truth; the patients resented the fact that I had my own dressing-gown and slippers, incidentally from Marks & Spencers, but still my own and not lent to me by the hospital. I was not amused and decided that somehow I must break down the walls of Coventry where they had sent me. There was not much for me to do in this ward when I was not reading or when they were talking among themselves; but after a day or two the nurses set us to work. They put the chairs in a circle and we were asked to sit there and roll bandages. The patients almost drew their nighties aside when I sat down but I waited my opportunity. Then greatly daring, I asked the ringleader if I could look at her knitting pattern. There was a deathly hush but she handed it to me. I made some pleasant remark and at last she answered. Then the others joined in and it was OK, I was accepted. In the meantime I had achieved modest notoriety in another direction. While we were talking one day, I told three or four of the women which sex I thought their children would be. In due course it happened that I was right in each case. They were all very impressed and I had to go round the ward and give my opinion to each one. Even the nurses and the two sisters were interested as I prophesied correctly in most cases. I had a theory which I still have and this was proved correct in about 80% of my guesses.

There were about 20 of us in the ante-natal ward, and one by one they left us and went 'upstairs'; in other words, they had their babies and were put in one of the small rooms which usually held three beds. When my turn came, three days late on 1st November, I was put in a room with Mrs Wardley from Ipswich and Mrs Hobbs from London. Mrs Wardley looked like Kay Kendall and her 11 lb baby boy seemed incongruous, until we learned that she was married to a policeman. We could just imagine him in a helmet. Mrs Hobbs was 18 and quite bewildered that she had produced a tiny baby girl. Neither of them had any idea about names, so, with their approval, I named them both. Thus somewhere in the world there are presumably two people just over 40, who are strange to me but in whom I have an interest; and their names are Heather Hobbs and Martin Wardley.

I was in the Sunnyside Maternity Home for a further two weeks, and I don't think I have ever laughed so much and so often before or since. One source of amusement to us was the arguments and disagreements, not to say fights, between the two teams of nurses from London and Ipswich. All their techniques and methods and ideas seemed diametrically opposite, and they didn't hesitate to thrash things out at the tops of their voices and in front of the patients. Directly after my baby was born in the early hours of the morning, the two Sisters stood one each side of me and argued vehemently as to whether I should have 'just one tiny stitch' or no stitch at all. I couldn't have cared less and I lay there giggling hysterically; I had one stitch. We were supposed to stay put in our own rooms, but everyone was always wandering about and talking and laughing and joking in their different dialects and then tearing back to their rooms when they heard any of the staff coming upstairs.

I only had two visitors while I was there. My mother came on one occasion and Harvey came down for one weekend. We called the baby Yvonne Daphne but she was always know as 'Bobsa'. When we were coming home my mother hired a car and Wookey held the baby girl on her lap as we drove back to the bungalow.

Mother had found another place for us to stay and in due course we moved to Queen's Farm, which was quite a long way further up Huntley Road towards the school. It was a long, low, white building with mauve curtains at all the windows and it looked at first sight picturesque and inviting, but we discovered that its main attraction was the outside. 'Farm' proved to be a courtesy title as there was little land and very few animals. We were given three rooms. My mother and Wookey had a fairly big bedroom, but mine just held a single bed and the baby's cot. Our sitting-room was hardly more than a cupboard with only room for a small table and two chairs and the fireplace. There were two doors opening at each side so that a fierce draught blew through and we had to keep the cot on the table. As we cooked on the open fire by means of trivets, our diet had to be even simpler than the restrictions of wartime dictated. One advantage was that we could find some entertainment by looking out of the window. There was little else we could do apart from read or perhaps knit, providing we could find some old garment to unravel. I bought a tiny zinc bath for the baby and this I had to use for the washing after I had boiled small quantities of water on the fire.

Wookey was quite happy; she made lots of little friends and was getting on very well at school. When she was 4 years and 8 months old, I remember that she read the headline on the newspaper which said: *Petain says 'No' to Japan*. The farm belonged to an elderly woman and her very eccentric daughter whose habits left much to be desired. One of her less offensive habits was to shake filthy rugs out of an upper window so that the dirt fell all over the pram and the sleeping baby.

We tried to make the best of our stay there but eventually in the spring of 1941 we made an effort to find somewhere more suitable. We were lucky indeed, and we moved into Stone End Farm which was on the same main road between the bungalow and Queen's Farm. This was a beautiful red brick, oak-beamed house; it was surrounded by a lovely garden with the farm beyond. In this big house there was plenty of room for us and for Mr and Mrs Davis and their two daughters. They all treated us wonderfully well, and Maggie, their maid, was friendly and helpful. We had three very large rooms. It was delightful. Wookey could play in the garden and I could put the baby out in her pram on the lawn. The two Springer Spaniel dogs, Patsy and Judy, would sit one each side of the pram and woe betide any stranger who came near it. We were able to cook and do the washing in the kitchen, and Mr Davis would bring us big baskets of logs for our sitting-room fire. Apart from being away from home, we couldn't have been happier.

During all the time we stayed in Churcham I went to dances with my brother-in-law. He loved dancing and despite appearances to the contrary, he was an accomplished performer. Hilda did not care for dancing and he was glad to find that I was willing to go; moreover being small, I suited him well enough. I would lift up my long dance dress and climb into the old brown Austin among the cabbages and carrots and the dried mud. Then off we banged and rattled into the surrounding blacked-out countryside. We were bound for some lonely village hall and there we danced in an atmosphere of simple gaiety amid the black-out material and the clinking school milk bottles and the heaps of gas masks which would never be used. I joined the Drama Section of the Women's Institute and was in a small one-act play which we gave at Churcham School. I made quite a hit, mainly I suspect because of the cockney accent which amused them, as it was so unfamiliar. These little adventures helped to lighten a routine of darkness, children and deprivation.

We stayed at Stone End Farm until the bombing quietened down and we came back to Beckenham in August 1941. It was thus that my younger daughter was nine months old before she entered her own home.

Wookey went back to Dartery House School, but not for long. The Headmistress, while acknowledging that Celia was a brilliant child, told me that she was also an unhappy child, and that the only member of her family that she loved was her baby sister. She suggested a boarding-school with a resident psychologist. Needless to say we were very indignant and were sure that there was no truth in the allegation. Consequently we took her away from Dartery House and sent her to Mason's Hillstate School in Bromley. From then on there was no suspicion that she was not a normally happy child.

The autumn and winter of 1941 passed uneventfully by and one day in the spring of 1942, when I was sitting in the garden doing nothing in particular, Harvey suggested that I find myself a job. I was quite willing; many of my friends were still evacuated, my mother was there to look after the children, and my life had become dull and tiresome. Food was boring and scanty, our clothes were old and out of date, even knitting and needlework were impossible without wool and material. The days seemed to consist of dreary domestic trivialities, so I said — well yes, but it must be something helpful to the war effort. I found one or two advertisments in the newspaper and set off for London. I had one rather nice blue suit and I'd always been good with hats but I hadn't got any stockings. However, there was nothing unusual about the sight of bare legs in those frugal days. I went to a private agency and was sent to Great Cumberland Place to apply for some vague position in something called 'Services of Supply'; and that was how I found myself working for the

American Army.

As it was now June 1942, I had really got in 'under the counter'. I started work on the 6th floor of a block of some erstwhile luxury flats at No 2 Great Cumberland Place. I was engaged as a typist; shorthand was, I was glad to learn, unnecessary. For the first few weeks I worked for Major Max Emmanuel; he was Jewish and he was one of the few Americans I met that I really liked. Everything was fairly chaotic as may be imagined, but American efficiency soon began to smooth the path. Working in the office with me, but soon promoted, was a tall attractive lady called Marie Black. She obviously knew nothing about office work; she asked me to help her, and I taught her how to do a stencil. Not so long afterwards she became Lady Tedder. We only stayed in that building for a month or two as they had been preparing our permanent home in Duke Street. This was a building behind and belonging to Selfridge's, and was taken over by the US Army for the duration. The walls were six feet thick and the inside was roughly divided into various-sized offices. We were issued with elaborate Passes and the Military Police were always on duty at the door. I was allocated to the typing pool, but most of us were attached to a specific department. There were about 20 of us and our supervisors were Mrs Primmer and Miss Angel. A little later on when we began to learn the names of US equipment and vehicles, I named them the 'Prime Mover' and the 'Angle Dozer'.

The typing skill of the members of the pool varied quite a lot and as I was pretty fast and accurate, I was attached, together with a younger woman called Muriel Foster, to the 'Manifest Department'. Two men in that department, who had been in Shipping before the war, had to index the ships' manifests and bring them in to us to type stencils from dictation. We were also considered eligible to do 'Secret' work. All civilians were vetted and classified; some girls were allowed to do 'Confidental' work but others were only considered fit to deal with 'Restricted' documents. We had of course been warned very seriously about careless talk and enquiries were made into our families and background. Even so, although I very seldom went into a pub, I was often surprised at what I heard being discussed there, and in cafés and other public places. I was extremely careful and certainly wouldn't even have used the word 'Manifest' in public.

The men who worked with us were Frank Smith and Robert Deering. The four of us worked together and we went to coffee and tea together; Muriel with Frank and Robert with me. Muriel and Frank were friendly and worked well together. Robert and I also became friends but we gradually realized that our friendship was developing through respect into affection, and then into an even deeper relationship. This really began on 19th August 1943, which was my 35th birthday. Robert asked me to go for a meal with him and we just talked and learned about each other's lives. Robert was married and had one son. His marriage was not very happy and mine was even less so by this time. He wrote to me every day although we were working together;

sometimes I received more than one letter; he just wrote down what he wanted to say whenever it occurred to him to do so. They were beautiful letters but sad. Often while walking in the street, he would leave me briefly and return with a rose-bud or a bunch of violets. Thursday became our day and we usually managed to have that day off together. If it was cold or wet we went to the theatre and we saw some good plays in dark, bleak buildings; or we went to the cinema and I remember seeing *Casablanca, Double Indemnity,* and *Now Voyager.* When it was fine Robert showed me the towns and countryside to the north of London. He lived in Harrow, so it was an area he knew well, while I was a south-east Londoner and knew nothing of the north. We went to Beaconsfield, St. Albans, Gerrards Cross, Denham, Windsor, and other places which it was possible to reach on our day out. We were very happy. One day we went to West Wickham to see my father who was a jeweller, and Robert bought me a diamond ring. We knew we could do nothing decisive until the war was over, and we were content to wait.

In the meantime there had been some changes among the civilian personnel in Duke Street. In the early days it seemed that all the ladies of leisure who were free for some form of war service, 'joined the US Army'. The army was not fussy and scooped them all up. Some of these conscripts were rich and some were titled and several of them, like Lady Ashley's sister, lived permanently at the Ritz Hotel. They had an astonishing number of fur coats between them and they wore orchids in their buttonholes. It would be putting it mildly to say that they were passengers. While we ordinary women were taking memos or hitting a typewriter, they sat about in groups and talked and smoked. There were some efforts made to teach them filing but about ten minutes a day seemed to be their limit. They spent about an hour at tea or coffee, they came late in the morning and they left early at night. We got on with our work; we did not resent these ladies, this was war and life was different.

Finally, however, latent American discipline emerged and became aware, and these very decorative ladies vanished in a puff of their own cigarette smoke. The work went on. Typing ships' manifests may not sound exciting but it was important. It meant listing the contents of each US ship which came to Europe for the progress of the war, that is from the heaviest army vehicle to the smallest screw. This work had to be indexed and typed at great speed directly the manifest reached us and there was a deadline. There was no packing up at 5.30, it had to be finished. I was never actually driven home in a Jeep, but some people were. However, many was the night I arrived at Beckenham Junction to see the last bus disappearing. It was infuriating at the time to have to walk home 35 minutes in the black-out, but it never occurred to me that I might be hit over the head.

In the spring of 1944, although the skies were quiet, Harvey began again to be uneasy and he dropped vague hints of trouble to come. I paid little heed; I was happy working for the US Army and my friendship with Robert was all that I could wish. I was sure that I could never have a more delightful and complete relationship with anyone else. Harvey was officer in charge of the Home Guard at Langley Court, and it wasn't until several months later that we realized that he had been instructed about the existence of the V-weapons and that it was a secret that he couldn't share with us. So it happened to us as to so many other people that one night the first Flying Bombs came to the south of England, and we were totally unprepared. Harvey explained what they were and said he had known about them for some time. I remember I had promised to take Bobsa to Kelsey Park the next day "to feed the ducks." But there was no chance of that, Harvey packed my mother and the children off to Gloucester straight away and my mother was only too glad to go; she was very frightened by this time. Wookey was then eight and Bobsa was three and a half. After they had gone, Harvey said: "Well, I'm going to sleep in the shelters at Langley Court. If you've got any sense, you'll get out of here and go north of London somewhere."

On the following day I went back to work and explained the situation to Robert. He said: "We'll go together." In wartime decisions are made very quickly. He left home the next morning, not to return for some time, and I brought a small case up to London with me. We spent the whole day tramping the streets north of London, but found nowhere to stay. Finally, and now in desperation, we took a train from Marylebone to Uxbridge. We walked along the main road that bordered the RAF station. It was getting late and was already dusk. We enquired at one of the tall terraced houses to which we had been directed by an official at the railway station. We had meant to ask for two rooms. We had had no intention of posing as husband and wife, but before we could make this known, we were offered one small room which was all they had free. Thus there began a false existence which was imposed on us by circumstances. That night as we lay in a narrow bed and watched one or two stray V1s pass over, we wondered too about our safety.

We were very comfortable in Hillingdon Road — especially when we moved into a larger room — and we liked Mrs G. and her husband very much. There was a little problem about Ration Books, for of course I couldn't use mine; but we managed quite well. We had our breakfast in the Corner House when we got to Oxford Street, and in the evening we either ate out or took something in with us. Every now and·then I travelled down to Beckenham and either used my Ration Book in that district or took some food out of my own cupboard.

We walked to Uxbridge station and travelled back and forth each day quite happily, though it was a longer journey and took forty-five minutes on the train. When we left Duke Street in the evening, we walked along Baker Street to the station. Many times when the Flying Bombs had begun to come over, they literally chased us the length of the street. If the one overhead was clanging along fairly slowly, we ran and ran, as I had never run before, so that we might reach the shelter of the station before the engine cut out. If it was flying quickly, we hung back, only to find another bomb was following on its tail and was over our heads again. We felt trapped in that long straight street. Sometimes the bombs followed the train and I silently hoped that when they came down we would not be in the underground part of the track. I would rather have been killed than buried. We arrived each evening at Uxbridge with grateful relief; the few Flying Bombs we did see there only served to make us more thankful for security until the morning.

When we finally left Hillingdon Road we discovered that Mr and Mrs G. had known we were not married almost from the beginning. Mr G. had said: "My dear, they are nice people and we like them both. It's none of our business."

My mother and the girls were happy enough in Churcham. They were staying with Mr and Mrs Sidney Smith at Duncombe House very near the school, and later on with Mrs Johns at Hendre House in Oakle Street. I went down to see them several times. Huntley Road was now a very dangerous thoroughfare between Gloucester and Hereford and the American vehicles screeched and pounded along there with very little respite for the people who lived along its margin. Wookey told me that the children nicknamed the tank carriers 'Long Bonnets' and 'Snub Noses'. The US soldiers called out to the children from these vehicles and threw them packets of chocolate, biscuits and chewing-gum as they passed, which was a great treat for them. My mother told me that she practically had to throw the children into the hedge sometimes, as there were still no paths and the road was very narrow.

Wookey was happy at school and they were both very popular for the little songs and recitations they performed, especially 'There's a hole in my Bucket', when Wookey aged 8 played the woman and Bobsa aged 3½, played the man. Wookey had a lot of friends; I remember Margaret Mack, the vicar's little girl, Jean Smith, daughter of a teacher, Jennifer Hughes, Gordon Lodge, and the triplets, Marigold, Iris and Primrose, evacuated there with their mother. I was missing the girls but I didn't want to stay in Gloucestershire with them. I travelled back quite willingly to the dangers of London and the security of Robert.

Robert and I had one short but delightful holiday during the summer. We spent three days at the Bell Hotel in Hurley. This lovely old inn by the Thames in the Berkshire countryside seemed to be a corner of a world we had almost forgotten. The inn was warm and comfortable and the food was delicious and showed no sign of rationing restrictions. One day in fact we overheard two Ministry of Food officials questioning the proprietors about how this was managed. I admit we didn't care very much. We were enjoying everything and were grateful for such wonders that came our way before we had to return so soon to our demanding and exacting work.

Some time during the autumn of 1944 the much talked about V2 weapons began to fall. They did not bother me as the V1s had done as they were fewer and much further between. There was no warning signal so unless you got a direct hit, you could ignore them. One morning, however, when we arrived in Duke Street, there was unusual activity. We could see that the public house right opposite the US building had indeed had a direct hit in the night and was a heap of rubble; all the inhabitants had been killed. I think it was called The Duke of York. Our building had survived almost intact on the outside and the MPs let us in. Once inside, however, we could not recognize it; all the walls and divisions between the offices had been swept away, leaving one enormous hall. Although part of the upstairs was very dangerous and out of bounds, they let us go up the now silent escalator to the office where I was working at that time. Someone said to me: "If that had fallen during the day, you wouldn't be here now!" And I saw that right across my desk lay a huge wooden beam. We collected what belongings we could and were then directed to Bryanston Square where we took possession of No 6, and we stayed there for 6 weeks while Duke Street was being repaired.

Sometimes Robert went home to Harrow to see his wife and son. She knew about me and Robert answered all her questions and helped her to try to understand the situation. She made no fuss but she worked on his kindly nature when it was possible in the hope that he would eventually return.

We stayed at Uxbridge for nine months. We were still happy together but we had both begun to be restless. Ours had become an uneasy and unnatural existence and we missed our children. Mine came home in March 1945 so I left Uxbridge and returned to them. Robert decided to get a flat in Beckenham. Strangely enough I was against this and would rather he had gone back to Harrow, not because I wanted us to part, far from it, but because I felt it would be happier for him and I was afraid he would be lonely. I was proved to be right. We travelled together and I often spent the evening with him but I had to leave him at last and I knew he would not be content for long in a strange place among strange people.

The war ended and any hopes we had had ended with it. We were both married and Robert had no job to go to. We left the Americans to tidy up and go back home, and inevitably Robert went home too. In spite of our parting, nobody lived happily ever after, but then perhaps nobody ever does.

It is not possible to write about a war in isolation. Sometimes it becomes entangled with life and sometimes its sights and sounds merely serve as a backcloth against which life is played. It was so with me. As I stood in the Blake Recreation Ground in West Wickham, and watched my two little girls happily joining in the VE Day party, I felt no great relief or joy, just a sense of something having passed which left me silent and waiting.

Life with the ATS

by Josephine Birchenough

Ever since I could remember I had wanted to be in the Army. The fact that I was a girl had not concerned me. My father had taught me a good deal of the noble art of self-defence before I was 5, and he had also taught me a lot of Army folklore — snippets from the Drill Book, how to lay out kit, how to salute, how to slow march. My father had served as a too-young man in South Africa in 1900-1901 and all through the First War, but for 7 years in the 1920s he was without a regular job and my mother was the wage-earner. So I spent a good deal of time with my father, and he taught me much of the soldier's trade, together with the tales, slang and songs that are part of the great oral tradition of the British Other Ranks.

So, when I was 18 and a women's auxiliary for the Territorial Army was being formed, I joined, in spite of fairly active resistance from my mother. The officers were 'county' ladies very largely associated with the Guides, and the odd one of two who had been FANYs in the Great War. There were four trades available to us other ranks ('Volunteer' was the name of the rank in which we rejoiced) and I, as I had just finished my training as a shorthand typist, went in as a clerk. A friend of mine who was a member of a 'county' family, to her great credit, went in as a cook, and rose to the dizzy heights of Sergeant.

As Territorials before the war, we used to go down to the Drill Hall a couple of nights a week, where chaos reigned. No one really knew what we were supposed to be doing (men and women alike). Military items were issued on a 'lucky dip' basis, and you turned up wearing such items as had been issued to you. The men at one stage were mainly equipped with a 'housewife' and a 'cap, comforter'. That parade evening still stands out in my memory as one of the most hilarious of my life — a thousand things you can do with a 'cap, comforter'. (For the uninitiated, a 'housewife' is a fabric roll containing needles, thread, etc., for doing minor repairs, and a 'cap, comforter' is a tube of knitted material about 9 inches wide and a couple of feet long, joined at either end. You could either use it as a scarf or, with one end pushed through, as a sort of woolly hat.)

We women were introduced to the gentle art of marching drill, the instructions echoing strangely over the 13 years since I had first learned to put my thumbs in line with the seams of my trousers, and 'longest way up, shortest way down' (which is the shorthand way of teaching the correct way to salute). The art of 'forming fours' was not required now that we drilled in threes, but it was no problem to my father, as that was how they had done it when he was in the Mounted Infantry in South Africa all those years earlier. Those of us destined (I nearly wrote 'doomed') for the paper war, did additional training in military office routines and had the usual initiation ceremony. When I went home after the first evening, my father asked me what we had been doing. When I started to tell him "Amending King's Regulations," he knew that I was following in his footsteps, since, when he was in South Africa, as one of the few literates in his battalion he had done it too.

By the time we went to camp in August 1939 we were a pretty motley crew, the girls pretty well fully kitted out (although only the parts that showed); but the men had a depressing variety of fatigues, First War uniforms, oddly-shaped battledress and a few bits and pieces left over from OTC days. Our ex-Guide officers were in their element, preparing us for camp and showing us how to barrack the beds, but it was my father again who showed me how to make a warm bed which didn't fall apart. He also showed me how to make a charpoy out of a sack and some sticks, but I have never needed to use that skill.

The unit to which I was attached was a Yeomanry Bn. of the Royal Artillery. A good many of the men had joined because the dress uniform included spurs and a triangular piece of interlocking chain called a 'burnish' on the shoulders — reminders of their horseback days. It came as a nasty shock when they got oddments of hand-me-down khaki and a couple of museum-piece field guns.

Our camp was at Shoreham-by-Sea for a fortnight from the beginning of August and it rained nearly all the time. We had almost nothing to do during the day, apart from the cooks, who were fully occupied coping with the Soya stoves which I am sure they had never envisaged even in their wildest dreams. The evenings were different, though. There were 17 of us girls and about 1,700 men!

We came back from camp the middle Sunday in August. It so happened that I was between jobs. My previous employer had not been prepared to allow me to have time off to go to camp, so I gave him notice and quit. I got another job arranging to start on 1st September. That was a Friday and so we agreed that I should start the following Monday! Even though it should have been obvious to us, we didn't *really* expect there to be a war. Anyway, I was at a loose end for a fortnight and used to go down to the TA office daily to work in a voluntary capacity. KRs had been amended up to date long ago, so had the FSPB (Field Service Pocket Book) and all the Training Manuals.

Gradually the flood of paper built up and the telephone lines to various headquarters became jammed. It was pathetic. The bumbling easy-going, historic, peacetime routine was being rudely strangled by the onward rush of events, and the machine was totally unable to cope with it. The 'county' ladies sank without trace. I used to say that it would be a good idea to bring Army office routine screaming and yelling into the nineteenth century!

We soldiered on and those of us who had been working all week decided to take a breather at the weekend. My sister and I went dancing on the Saturday night and agreed with our boy-friends to have a day out on the river on the Sunday, as we did most Sundays. The boys would come and collect us about 11 a.m. They were a few minutes early because they wanted to hear what the Prime Minister had to say. We listened, our worst fears were confirmed, I had a little weep, and we all went off for our day on the river. It was a glorious day. We got very drunk.

I turned up at the TA office on the Monday morning and wrote myself a call-up notice dating from 1st Sept 1939, along with many hundred of others. My paper war had started. I had joined for 'General' Service anywhere, but my mother exercised her right, as I was under 21, to have me transferred to 'local' service which meant that, after a few weeks I had to report at the local barracks, originally the regimental depot, but now the Infantry Training Centre of the local county infantry regiment of whom my father remarked disparagingly that their motto was 'Thou shalt not kill'. And awful come-down for me initially; but I was ordered to report to the Adjutant's office for duty as the Adjutant's Secretary. I had to deal with all Secret, Security and Confidential matters, was given a couple of 'protection' stripes and was looked after by the Adjutant's runner, a most charming elderly recalled reservist right at the end of this time with the biggest chestful of medals I have ever seen outside the top brass and Royal family. He had the MM and the DSM, also their equivalents from the French and Belgians, but I could never get him to tell me about the exploit(s) which gave rise to them.

My two ATS colleagues, the CO's secretary and the Orderly Room Corporal and I rapidly beat the regimental office work into shape, respecting but feeling sorry for the peacetime officers to whom the avalanche of paper came as a horrid and unwelcome shock for which they were both unprepared and untrained. We worked happily and hard. The regiment still kept the peacetime tradition of games on Wednesday afternoons and we used to retire each week to the Barrack Field for fierce games of mixed hockey. The three office corporals were the main attackers of the forward line.

Efforts were made in the early days of the war to send entertainers to the barracks. Most of them were so embarrassingly awful that some of us who were on the permanent staff at the barracks decided that we couldn't do any worse and ought to put on a few shows. Some of the recruits were professional or good amateur entertainers. Some of the girls were prepared to sing and dance, and we had some first-class musicians, as the 'permanent staff' included assorted bandsmen from both the two regular battalion bands which had been 'disbanded'. It finally shook down to a group of half a dozen of us, who sparked ideas off each other. We wrote (mainly in the 'Sally Ann' — Salvation Army canteen), scored, dressed and performed a good many excellent shows, before the serious business of war really started to bite. The concert party succumbed eventually to an influx of officers' wives, who wanted to take over and do it themselves. We used a few of them in one of our shows, and then they said they would do the next one themselves, but it never materialized.

The 'Phoney War' had given us the opportunity to organize the Army paper work more in accordance with mid-twentieth-century practices, and going to the office in the Army was very similar to working in a civilian office except that you took your hockey stick to work on Wednesdays; you didn't need to wonder what to wear; and you had to salute for your pay on Fridays.

Then our world fell apart. The men on the Continent were retreating to the Channel ports, the King asked us to join in a national day of prayer and the troops came home, tired and dirty, to be accommodated in makeshift camps all over our part of the country, and kept incommunicado while any Fifth Columnists were identified and removed. Suddenly there was feverish activity. I worked from 8 a.m. until 10 or 11 p.m.; it was really just working, eating and sleeping. As the strain began to tell, we all started to take an hour or so off in the middle of the day to go swimming. At least one of the senior officers cracked under the strain. 'My' dear Adjutant had been posted shortly before, and his replacement was an opinionated bad-tempered b---, I found him extremely difficult to work with. Towards the end of the period of 'flap', his temper finally broke and he threw a glass ashtray at me. It missed, but I burst into floods of tears, the strain being broken for me too, and I raced across to the 'Attery' swearing to my Sergeant-Major that I utterly refused to go back to that b---- ever again. My mother insisted that I leave the Army immediately! She could! I was not yet 21, and we were only volunteers anyway! So I took immediate discharge, and never *did* go back to that b----!

I had only been out of the Army for about a fortnight, when women had to register for war work. I went along (suffering, according to the doctor, from 'nervous debility') and signed up. I was told to find work of national importance, or they would direct me. Strangely enough I looked forward to being 'directed' away from my mother's overpowering influence. In the meantime, I took the first job offered, as secretary in a little firm of auctioneers, estate agents and valuers, in the market square of our small country town. That 12 months was fairly uneventful, workwise. We held regular auctions (about one a month) and it was my job to act as auctioneer's clerk, sorting out people's bills, etc., at the end of the period of selling. We sold everything — junk, fine historic silver and beautiful furniture, including some Chippindale sets of chairs authenticated with the original bills! I never had to lot up a herd of cows, though!

Socially, however, that year (1941) held many changes for me. When I was recovering from my 'nervous debility', my mother and I had gone up to

Blackpool for a few days at the seaside (that being almost the only part of the coast known to us where we *could* go). We hadn't been in the boarding house for more than a day or so when it was taken over as officers' accommodation for the Polish Air Force. They came in, charming, polished, attractive Europeans, speaking little or no English, in their hundreds. How lucky those of us were who were 21 and spoke French! I sorted myself out a most desirable character — Bronek — who was one of the heroes of the Polish Warsaw Squadron (later known as 303), who had already won the Polish equivalant of the VC. My mother sorted *herself* out one of the more senior Colonels of the Polish Air Force. My friendship with Bronek lasted all through the rest of the war, even though he was shot down and nearly killed in 1942. He used to come to our home for leave and often bring friends — the house sometimes seemed full to the bursting with Polish officers. Although we were extremely fond of each other and, of course, were living together, there was never any hope of us marrying, as he intended to go back to Poland after the war to 'rebuild'. His hopes must have been sadly shattered at the way the British abandoned the Poles after the war when the personal hopes of close alliance were so high.

After about 12 months at the auctioneers I received a demand to go for interview for 'war-work'. When I got there, I was greeted with, "We don't want you, we are looking for bus conductors." I rather fancied myself dishing out tickets and doing the old "Pass right down inside," but my parents were furious. "We didn't see to it that you had a good education to end up as a bus conductor!" So, a certain number of acrimonious exchanges resulted in the digging up of the fact that, when I left school in 1937, I had been in the VIth form at the local High School, doing Higher School Certificate Chemistry and Maths. This fact, which should have been elicited by my interviewer but wasn't, got my name put on the Scientific and Technical Register. Within a very short time I was called for interview in Cambridge. As I was a very well-qualified shorthand typist I naturally thought that these were the skills for which I was being called, and trotted off to Cambridge in a tailored 2-piece navy blue suit, a frilly blouse, a silver fox fur (which I had bought at the aution rooms for £2) and a saucy little hat. I was a little surprised when the interviewers started talking about Chemistry, a subject I had not even thought of since leaving school 5 years before. Disappointed that there was no hope of making a career in that subject I had put it right into the back of my mind. However, I dredged up sufficient elementary Chemistry from the recesses of my memory to satisfy the interviewers, and they told me to go home and I would be hearing from them — and did I have any preference as between Nottingham and Leyland. I said Leyland would be easiest as it was very close to my father's old home at Chorley and we still had friends there who had known my father since boyhood, who could put me up.

Literally within a few days I got a letter asking me to report to such and such a factory in Leyland at such and such a time and date. We contacted the

Chorley friends who could accommodate me for a couple of days or even a week or so, while I attended (as I thought) a training course, *but*, when I got to the Leyland factory they weighed and measured me, gave me the Official Secrets Act to sign, a lab coat to wear, and took me down to the labs to start work! And there I stayed till the end of the war. The old family friends were very good and long-suffering and I lived there for a couple of years, being compelled to leave ultimately because of unacceptable attentions by (a) the local Inspecter of Police and (b) my landlord, my father's friend and contemporary! The airs some men give themselves!

So, for the last year or so of the war I lived in a hutted camp run by the YWCA for female factory workers, in one of the 'non-industrial' blocks, and thoroughly enjoyed myself. We used to have a drama group and I was in a couple of plays, the last being *Nine Till Six*, an all-women play about a dress shop. The war was coming to an end and it was a race between that and the production of the play. The war won, and I stayed over for a few extra days at the YWCA to do the play as I had one of the crucial parts.

Chorley

Life in Chorley was, in 1942, little affected by the war, except that most of the fit young men had already left. We had a most active social life. A Girls' Training Corps was formed, and, on the basis of my previous Army service, I was appointed an officer. We used to take part in processions, including the Mayor's Walking Day (a procession on the Sunday after 9th November, when the newly-appointed Mayor processed round the town, accompanied by anyone who wished him well). All processions in Chorley used to go (and for all I know still do) down the wide main street (called Market Street), round the Big Lamp (which is no longer there) and back down the other side of the street. Thus it was inevitable that the band(s) coming up the street would meet head-on with the band(s) going down. The cacophony could be unbelievable; as the bands included the local stalwarts The Besses o' The Barn, Leyland Motors, Fodens, Preston Police and the local Army Cadets whose band was first-rate. Occasionally one or other of my uncles, aunts or cousins would catch sight of me in the procession and hail me with 'Nay, there's our Alf's Joy' with a certain amount of pride, as there was an indication of some social standing if you 'walked with the Mayor'. The Girls' Training Corps had many social events, often in conjunction with the Army Cadets, not only in Chorley but in the other places around, and I can recall many wonderful sausage and mash and potato pie suppers.

Even though it was wartime, the Civil Service liked its people to keep on working to improve their academic qualifications, even those of us who were only there for the duration. Most of us from the labs used to go to night school at the Harris Institute in Preston. this was about 5 miles from Leyland, and as I normally used to cycle to work from Chorley to Leyland (also about 5 miles), it meant a ride home of between 9 and 10 miles in the black-out afterwards. We were used to cycling in the black-out and, being in our 20s and very fit, we never thought twice about it. We used to go to Preston and Wigan and even to Manchester for concerts and the theatre. The shows at 't' Hippo' (the Hippodrome in Preston) were wonderful, all the best artistes in the country being then engaged in touring. We saw plays, the ballet, everything. The Liverpool Phil. used to give concerts in the baths. The annual Chorley Messiah used to take place on a Sunday afternoon in the largest cinema in the town, with singers from all the local church and chapel choirs, and soloists of repute. Isobel Baillie (a local girl and related to my father's step-mother) was a frequent visitor, and it was on these occasions that I first thrilled to the magnificent voice of Kathleen Ferrier (also almost a local girl), when she was still a relatively unknown semi-pro and working, I believe as a telephonist in Blackburn. Sitting and singing the Messiah in a cinema on a Sunday in wartime Lancashire was an unforgettable experience. The audience was expected to join in the better-known choruses.

Living at the foot of the Pennines, we were members of the YHA and used to go off walking or cycling on holiday weekends in pairs or groups of friends. I have walked many hundreds of miles with my Welsh friend, Nancy Jones. We walked all over the Lake District, the North Pennines and North Wales. By the end of the war, we had stayed in a high proportion of the Youth Hostels in NW England. We usually used to go on the factory bus after work on Saturday, to whatever town the bus was going, and walk to a hostel during the afternoon, stay the night there, walk most of Sunday, and catch a bus or train home in the evening. The Double Summer-Time was helpful, as it meant that we could often walk in the light until 10 p.m. or after. The heat of the day was usually about 3 p.m., when we could rest up for an hour and have tea somewhere. We discovered that many of the country inns in the mountains were mysteriously well supplied with goodies and, although the front door might be shut out of licensing hours, the back door was open. We rarely used to bother to take swimming costumes with us, and I have had many a magnificent nude swim in the cold waters of the high lakes and tarns. I suppose it was foolish because we were completely alone, but both Nancy and I could swim extremely strongly and both had our life-saving Bronze Medallions.

Part of my job in Lancashire entailed collecting samples of products made at various local factories on a variety of government contracts. This entailed visiting not only the other factories in Leyland, but in Preston, Southport, Leigh and Shaw (near Oldham). Those sampling days were a delight and very much regarded as a bonus. You got your travelling paid *and* a subsistence allowance. Preston, however, was something of a nightmare. The factory we used to visit made polish in the slummier part of Preston (now demolished). Because of the volatile nature of the solvents used, there was no heating, and in the winter the women workers used to tie newspaper and brown paper round their arms, legs and body with string to keep out the cold.

They looked like badly-packed parcels.

Very early in my career in the Lancashire factories I realized that the natives were right to wear clogs and boiler suits (particularly as neither of them was on coupons) and I, too, equipped myself as a native, although when I went out sampling I also wore my blazer with the badge of one of our leading girls' schools. The hundreds of people I met in the factories of wartime Lancashire opened my eyes to a world hitherto entirely unknown, and introduced me to social and political ideas which would never have come my way in the normal course of events.

We had little experience of bombing, etc. I had been in both the factory fire brigade (where I had learned to erect a stand-pipe and that 'the female goes to the fire' — a jingle which tells you which way round to feed out the hose-pipe) and the street fire-watching group. I was a member of the display team which went around demonstrating how to put out incendiary bombs with a stirrup pump. But the only time a bomb was dropped on Chorley, I happened to be home on leave! We had a buzz-bomb too — just one managed to get over the Pennines and come pop-popping overhead as we were going home in the factory bus one day. We all agreed that, yes, it did sound just like a 2-stroke motor bike. But it passed overhead and I think it probably landed harmlessly in the Fylde. However, I had decided to crown my efforts at night school by taking Inter BSc, partly in Wigan, where I had done the theory papers, but the practical I would do at the Examination Halls in London, near the Albert Hall. I was not to know that that was going to be the start of the V2s, and that my titrations were going to be interrupted with visits to the shelters. Once I was just coming up to the end-point, and so I took a reading, in case my hand shook and the next drop should become several. There was a young nun doing the exam just near me, and when we were in the shelters, she took out her rosary. All the rest of us, who didn't have her training or inner resources, envied her. When I got back to Lancashire, they asked me what the set titration had been and when I told them, they merely reacted 'lucky devil' because it was one we did several times a day, day in, day out! No one was interested in the fact that I heard several V2s landing uncomfortably close. The building had shaken with some of them. I got a distinction in that exam!

As the war drew to a close, Bronek and I said goodbye and we never saw or heard of each other again. We had a big celebration on VE day. I cycled about 40 miles to the factory where a friend was and we had a fantastic party, with home-made fireworks (they were pyrotechnics experts). But of course we went back to work within a few days. The war in the Far East was very much 'with us' as our factory was producing items for that theatre of war.

VJ day came with something of a small riot in the middle of the night. The Yanks in the camp up the road came roaring down to our hutted camp and tried to climb over the gates. Our girls, who had precious little time for the Yanks, went out to support our decrepit night-watchman and to repel the boarders. Cross Geordies and Irishwomen in curlers and dressing-gowns armed with hairbrushes proved more than a match for the might of the US forces! We had a party the next night and started to make arrangements to go home, although I remained a few days to appear in the play. Production ceased in the factories immediately, and we completed our tests, cleaned the apparatus down, dis-assembled it, packed it all away, and left within a few days, leaving behind us the Emergency Water Tank outside the lab doors where we had swum in the summer and skated or slid in the winter, and the little factory rail trolley which had been one our playthings, and of which we took a photograph when the rule about taking photographs inside the factory was relaxed.

We said goodbye to the birch wood at the bottom of the factory field, Neddy Springs, the spring field where the wild watercress grew, the wild moors where the cottongrass blew and insectivorous plants grew above the treeline, the unbelievably beautiful sunsets, the quiet roads occupied by cyclists and heavy Army tanks on trial, the curious whisper as hundreds of clogs moved on the platform as the factory train came in, thick toast liberally spread with jam at the Harris canteen and the potato fritters which used to be cooked to perfection in the chip shop outside the factory gates.

So we all went home and looked for peacetime jobs.

Josephine Birchenough, second left, middle row.

'Making Do'

By Muriel V. Searle

If asked to epitomize the essence of wartime living without mentioning evacuation or bombing, one might well sum it up in two words: making do.

Making do when rationed food was too precious to waste; making do with clothes we would now give away to a jumble sale; making do at home, at school and at work. The Victorians' creed of waste not, want not, was revived for the duration, in almost everything.

Who now remembers public pig-swill bins, placed at strategic points in villages and country towns? Any table leftings and discarded peelings, apart from bones, should not be thrown away, but be kept back and taken to the nearest pig-swill bin. Periodically they were emptied and the contents taken to farms for helping out fodder supplies, for agriculture as well as arms was part of the salvation of the nation. As a Victorian rhyme, topically revived, reminded people:

> Dearly beloved brethren,
> Don't you think it a sin,
> That when you peel potatoes
> You throw away the skin?
> For skin feeds pigs,
> And pigs feed you.
> Dearly beloved brethren,
> Isn't this quite true?

Few modern schoolchildren know that their parents, when young, if living in a country district, were sometimes encouraged to go out with bags and baskets to pick scarlet rose hips from the autumn hedgerows. Rose hips, when liquidized into rose hip syrup, were a rich source of the vitamins that were lacking in an austerity rationed diet. Children therefore helped keep up supplies, taking their pickings to some official point to be weighed, and paid for in a few pence a pound as extra pocket-money.

Dried everything was the order of the day, including dried potatoes and dried egg. Dried egg when put to cook by itself formed a sickly and unsavoury looking mess which only people desperately short of the real thing could consider eating, but it had its uses in cooking and baking where fresh eggs could not be spared; the ration for an adult was sometimes as little as just one egg a week. Dried milk looked equally nauseating, but it was again suitable for cooking.

Potatoes were sometimes so scarce that every unused scrap must be kept back and used next day for old-fashioned bubble-and-squeak, a frying-pan dish of yesterday's boiled potatoes with left-over greens or cabbage, forked into a pancake-like thin mash in the pan; its name came from its characteristic of bubbling up and subsiding with little fatty squeaks in the heat. Potato pancakes were similar, but made of potato leftings alone. Mashed into a thin pancake spread evenly over a frying-pan, a potato pancake when lightly browned was so delicious as to be a meal in its own right, especially if fried in dripping. Dripping was also very tasty as a substitute for meat spreads; solidified after pouring from the baking tin of the Sunday joint, and therefore beautifully meat flavoured, dripping was spread on plain bread or toast, with the delicious jelly found at the bottom of the bowl put on top for additional flavour.

Even yesterday's tea dregs, left in the teapot, had uses which had not been much practised since Queen Victoria's day. Tea had been grandmother's favourite dye; now it was resurrected by housewives of the 1940s. Several days' tea dregs were enough when poured into a bowl to turn discoloured curtains into a more convincing beige shade; the more tea was used, the deeper the shade. 'Whites' to be dyed were left in the tea for several hours, or overnight, rinsed out, then dyed again until the desired colour was reached. One mother known to this writer equipped her child with a bathing costume for school swimming lessons by adding a gusset to the bottom of an old school vest, to form leg pieces, then dying it in tea for a beige effect, she being unable to afford either money or clothing coupons for a non-essential item.

In season, blackberry juice also made a good dye, though inclined to give a navy blue rather than crimson colour; this was a very fast dye, almost impossible to wash out if accidentally spilled.

Refrigeration in private houses, and even in shops, was almost unknown, yet milk was too precious to lose through going off in warm weather, or through being fly-infected. To keep a bottle cool, a housewife stood it overnight in a basin or saucepan of cold water. Women still used the old domestic art of making milk-tops to keep flies and insects off. A milk top was a circle of cotton from an old sheet or tablecloth, cut to about the size of a large handkerchief but round in shape, and hemmed at the edge. All around this outside edge, close together, glass beads taken from old necklaces were sewn for weighting the cover down. Haberdashery shops also sold cheap beads for this purpose, usually of deep green glass.

Thoroughly outdated sheets, worn so thin that 'you could shoot peas through them', in contemporary speech, were turned side-to-middle by cutting lengthways down the centre and stitching the two former outside edges to make a new middle section. When finally so worn that the frail cotton split at the least movement, the sheet was cut down into pillowcases, which in turn became handkerchiefs, which again became bandages.

Rag rugs were made the same way as in the poverty-stricken world of a century earlier. The technique was to take an old towel, or a sack cadged from a grocer, as backing, and onto it to sew at tightly spaced intervals long rows of narrow slivers of fabric cut to the size of rug wool, about three inches long by about a quarter-inch wide. This formed a drab but very hard wearing mat. Boys' outgrown shorts and jackets were ideal for rug making, along with tweed remnants of ladies' skirts and children's outer wear, or bargains from jumble sales.

Women also knitted smaller mats from cheap coarse dishcloth cotton, whose pale shade was again made more practicable by dyeing in tea or stewed fruit juices.

Clothes must never be thrown away, but cut down or adapted. Skirts were reversed by undoing their seams and restitching them with the former inside, being in good condition, now on the outside. The writer's little mother, a trained dressmaker, once cut ten inches off the bottom of a coat handed on from a tall sister-in-law, and made herself a smart matching hat from this excess fabric. Her millinery consisted of covering a large hollow circle of stiff cardboard with material to form a wide brim, attaching this to a simple crown. The resulting matching outfit was both warm and smart.

A child's scarf could be turned into a winter pixie hood by folding it across at the centre and stitching down one of the sides to make a hood.

Women's dresses were cut down for their children, and the leftings hemmed as matching handkerchiefs. It paid to be a good dressmaker when all the money in the bank would not buy a dress unless one had the right number of clothing coupons as well.

Parachute silk, from enemy chutes found over Europe, or from duds withdrawn from service, was greatly prized for its beautiful quality, silky texture, and exquisite hang. Lucky was the bride who was able to acquire a few yards off a parachute to make her wedding gown. Sentiment rarely allowed her to keep it, however; this lovely material was too precious. The full length skirt was cut to a more practicable Sunday-best length, and the resulting cuttings used for perhaps a new blouse or for underclothes; the latter were a godsend, for normally lingerie had to 'go to pot' to conserve coupons for outer respectability.

Hair snoods came into fashion, initially as a necessity for containing the long floppy hair styles which came into vogue just when they were most impractical, as women took men's places in factories and on work benches, where loose hair was a real danger in the locality of moving machinery. Inevitably the snood — a giant hairnet of coarse mesh, usually in bright colours — graduated into a fashion accessory, setting crochet hooks flying among those who appreciated that make-it-yourself was cheaper than buying in a shop. Knitting also came back into full flight. At church and chapel women's meetings, free wool in regulation khaki was distributed to members for making what one lady nicknamed 'shocks for sholdjers' — socks for soldiers. Garment after garment flew off these ladies' needles, handed in at the next meeting in exchange for another allocation of khaki wool. They had three standard choices to make: balaclava helmets, scarves, or socks. Schoolgirls able to cope with simple knitting were set to make scarves, or to knit squares from their mothers' oddments of wool in any available colour; these were made up at school into blankets for refugees, similar to modern Oxfam blankets.

Bobble making, by winding wool scraps over the circular milk top with a centre hole which was then in use, swept the schools as a passing craze. Bobbles were added to everything from the point of a pixie hood to the fastener of a handbag, or the draw thread of a jumper, a harmless little diversion to lift the spirits in austere wartime.

Newspaper had more uses than to dispense information. Torn up papers screwed into twists acted as makeshift spills, which normally were sold as thin seven- or eight-inch long slivers of wood for igniting at one end over the fire or gas flame to save matches. Paper spills did the same job, but smelled abominably of soot, smoke, and scorching newsprint.

Twists of newspaper were much used by women as curlers, soft enough to be worn overnight as an alternative to rags over which the hair was twisted and then tied.

Sheets of newspaper held over the opening of a grate helped a fire to draw, by forcing the down draught back into the chimney. Brown paper served this job best, but newspaper was both cheaper and more readily available.

There was, of course, no such thing as TV, and many a family had no radio either. Winter evenings were therefore long and boring unless one entertained oneself. Simple games played by the fireside occupied these hours, mostly based on paper amusements such as making lists to see who could think of the greatest number of birds, flowers, insects, girls' names, boys' names, places beginning with one particular letter, names of stations, the shops of the local High Street in correct order; the possibilities were wide.

Old-fashioned faces-in-the-fire came back as families huddled indoors behind their black-out curtains, staring into the coals to discover shapes and forms made by the continual shifting of the black coal solids amid the glow of the embers.

A sheet hung at the wall made shadow play possible, forming outlines of beasts and birds with the hands, moving over the white ground as shadow creatures. A clever player could give a most realistic picture of a sheep opening its mouth, or a dog barking.

Outdoors, people were prodded by succeeding propaganda campaigns to give more time to vegetable gardening and less space to ornamental flowers. Dig for Victory was a typical example of a national drive, conducted mainly by newspaper advertisements and placards on hoardings. Producing one's own fruit and vegetables was both logical and laudable.

Many towns offered another alternative to eating off the weekly food allowance, by opening a Civic Kitchen, Civic Restaurant, or British Restaurant for the public. Spartan but wholesome dishes of the stew or sausage-and-mash variety were here on sale, along with cottage pie, steak pie, bacon and chips, mince and potato, and similar filling fare. Simple soups and puddings were also dished up, the latter laced with custard and mostly of the suet pudding kind. At only sixpence (2½p) a helping, a Civic Restaurant eased the strain on both pocket and ration book. In many towns they lasted into the first years of peace, until the austerity drive finally was abandoned in favour of normal living.

The 1940s were the last golden age of making do, when one ration coupon saved was as commendable as a half-crown (12½p) investing in a National Savings stamp towards the brighter future that sometimes seemed unlikely ever to dawn, as the war dragged on from weeks into months, and from months into nearly six years.

Police uniform of 1939-40
worn by Noel Searle of Catford Police Station.

Meeting the first Canadian Troops to arrive in England

by Brigadier Charles Edward Francis Turner, CBE, DSO

It was in December 1939 when I met the first Canadian Division to arrive in Scottish waters in a large convoy. They had come over here all set to fight the Germans. I was in charge of military movements in Aldershot and had obtained permission to meet them and travel back with them to the camps where they were to be stationed.

I spent a night in a small hotel in Glasgow and the next day went on board one of the small troopships which had been anchored up to the city docks. Finding a Brigadier Pearkes on board, I asked him and his Brigade Major to dine on shore with me later, and said that I would send a staff car for them. The troops were not to be disembarked until the next day.

The Brigadier was a First War VC, DSO and ME, and his Brigade Major proved to be none other than Major Simmonds, who was later to command the Canadian Army in Normandy. Brigadier Pearkes was to become a post war Canadian Minister of Defence.

It was a well kept secret, this arrival of such a vital convoy. As far as I can remember even the Lord Provost had not been told, but I confided to the hotel proprietor that I had invited two Canadian officers to dine, and he asked for an hour or so to prepare the meal to which, of course, I agreed.

We sat down to a fine repast with a handsome menu card (rationing had not yet taken toll of catering). In succession the name of each of the six courses began with the letters C then A followed by N, etc. It was a great success, and I gave the menu card to our senior guest.

Brigadier Pearkes had served in the Mounties and looked after his men very well. He was very amused when the Deputy Chief Constable of Glasgow came on board and told him that he had arranged for a large posse of police. We had to keep the men on board overnight and the police were afraid that they would jump over the ship's rail at low tide in the docks.

"Why," said my VC Brigadier, "are you afraid that the people of Glasgow will attack us and rush the ship?" One of the embarkation staff dropped a brick, at which they laughed and said they would put it into their War Diary. "Oh," said Captain X, "so you all speak English!"

I was up very early next morning to motor down the Clyde to the 'Tail of the Bank' at Greenock where the rest of the convoy of huge liners were lying at anchor. Trains were timed to leave from there every so often, and the disembarkation from these ships by lighter, fitted in with the departures, all meticulously worked out by Colonel Charles Napier, 'the Dome' at the War Office.

It was a crisp and sunny morning with clear visability, and the snow cladded Highlands picturesquely stood out to the north — all very impressive and historic. I have a particular memory of the 'Tail of the Bank' when I boarded a troopship on which the 22e (The Vingt Deuxieme), a regular Regiment of French Canadians, had sailed to Scotland. They came ashore in barges singing very melodiously.

I entrained with the Divisional Headquarters, and I remember four colourful characters — Lieutenant-Colonel Walford, the DAAG (Deputy Assistant Adjutant General), who rose to great heights in the Army; he also had a business in Montreal, and John Buchan, the author's son, who later became Lord Tweedsmuir when his father, the Governor-General, died. The senior Staff Officer named Turner (no relation) and the DADOS (Deputy Assistant Director of Ordnance Services) who called everbody "a Goddam son-of-a-gun."

Rations were available for the journey which all were to draw before entraining and orders were given for water-bottles to be filled. The Canadians did not see the necessity for this, and they did not bother. For the whole of their journey across Canada they had been supplied at every halt with food and drink from their cheering, hospitable, fellow-countrymen, cheering their heroes off to fight in foreign lands. Consequently the situation in this country came as a bit of a shock — over here life was different. They soon regretted not obeying orders!

I found myself supplying eats from a reserve I had with me to some of the hungry officers in my compartment. Drink was more of a problem. We pulled up in the black-out at York station in the middle of the night, and I tried to lay on with the LNER (London North Eastern Railway) officials some facilities for the water-bottles to be filled. No easy task for hundreds of men in the pitch black darkness, and certainly no lights were allowed to be used. It was not a comfortable journey for them by any means back to Aldershot, and what a relief to arrive the following day.

DISTINGUISHED SERVICE ORDER

Lieutenant-Colonel Charles Edward Francis TURNER, OBE (11966)
Corps of Royal Engineers

Lt-Col TURNER has been A.A. & Q.M.G. of the 7th Armoured Division during the whole advance from EL ALAMEIN to TUNISIA. His Division has been continuously in the front line.
He has made a point himself of visiting daily his forward Brigades and Units.

This has led him constantly through shellfire and through unchartered minefield. Often whilst visiting the 4th Light Armoured Brigade he has had to motor many miles across ground patrolled by enemy Armoured Fighting Vehicles. Thus, in addition to his arduous work in maintaining his Division during this long advance, he was constantly under enemy fire and subject to close-range enemy action.

His Division has taken part in every battle during this advance and has several times carried out large turning movements. The success of the Division has largely depended on his administrative ability. Without firsthand knowledge of the requirements of his forward units he could never have carried out this job successfully. Thanks, however, to his unselfish devotion to duty and determination whatever risk and difficulties to have a firsthand knowledge of the requirements of his forward units, his Division has never failed to carry our the task allotted to it.

London Gazette 14th October, 1943

*   *   *

To be an Additional *Commander of*
the Most Excellent Order of *the British Empire*

Lieutenant Colonel (temporary Colonel) Charles Edward Francis TURNER, DSO, OBE (11966)

Corps of Royal Engineers

HQ.FORTBASE had to open in SICILY with a much reduced staff due to shipping limitations. A heavy load of work and responsiblity fell on it immediately. This was borne in large measure by Col TURNER, the chief administrative staff officer. He overcame the difficulties very effectively and was unsparing of himself in competing with the exceptional volume of work.

London Gazette 23rd March, 1944

A Life on the Ocean Waves

by Iain Orr

Service Record:

HMS *King Alfred*	—	RNVR base at Hove training establishment February and March 1940
HMS *Clarkia* in command — Gwynne-Jones L/Cols. RNR	—	15th April-9th May 1940
HMS *King George V*	—	1st April, 1941-8th December, 1941
in command — W. Patterson, Captain RN		
XDO Kirkwall, Orkneys	—	8th December 1941-15th February 1942
in command — E. Hoyle, Captain RN		
HMS *Despatch* Commander in Command —	—	8th April, 1942 — 22nd April, 1942
M. Huntington-Whiteley	—	time only
Captain W. Leggat RN	—	25th April, 1942-June 1942 13th September, 1943 obtained Watchkeeping Cert 23rd June, 1942 — 25th September, 1943

FOTALI (Flag Officer Taranto, Adriatic, lower Italy)

M. McGregor, Rear Admiral	—	On the Staff as Fleet Base Security Officer (FBSO) from 15th November, 1943 to 15th March, 1944
Admiral C.E. Morgan		16th March, 1944 to 29th April, 1945
HMS *Fabius* (NOIC Trieste) in command Commander Guinness, RN,	—	Serving as Staff Officer Security from 3rd May to 31st August, 1945 acting Captain from 1st September-26th Nov 1945

under
C. Hulton, Acting Captain RN
and from 27th November, 1945-
28 Aug. 1946
Captain C. Noakes, RN, as War Booty Officer

*   *   *

SEAGOING SERVICE:

HMS *Clarkia* 15.4.1940 to 9.5.1940 Corvette

Built 7.8.1940
Tonnage: 925 tons
Complement: 85
L.o.a. 205 ft
Breadth — 33 ft
Draught — 14½ ft
Guns — 1 4 inch
          1 Pompon 20 mm
          Depth charge throwers & launchers
          Speed — 16 knots

HMS *King George V* — 1.4.1941 to 8.12.1941 Battleship

Completed 1940
Tonnage   35,000
Complement 1,900
Length — 745 ft, breadth 103 ft, Draught 27 ft 8 inches
Guns — 10 14-inch. 16 5.25-inch. 6 Pompons
          40 mm bofors 20 mm Oerlikans
Armour plating on waterline 16 inches
Speed — 30 knots 4 engine rooms 4 boiler rooms 4 screns?

HMS *Despatch* 8.4.1942 to 25.9.1943

Built — 1919
Tonnage 4,850 tons
Length — 445 ft w.t. 472 ft o.a.
Complement 469
Guns — 6 6-inch
          3 4-inch
Torpedoes — 12 tubes in 4 triple 21 inch

*   *   *

HMS *King Alfred*

At the outbreak of hostilities I was an accountant with a shipping company in Glasgow. I was married (having maintained the good old Scottish tradition of going across the border to England to carry her back).

After leaving the Glasgow Academy, I joined the Anchor Line, where my father had served for many years until his death in 1920.

When I was at school, I spent my holidays with a school friend whose father owned a 30ft yacht, and we sailed all the coast of Scotland including St Kilda, the inner and outer Hebrides and Orkney Islands, little did I know then that these islands were to be revisited during the war. Yachting is where I learned my seamanship and navigation. As the clouds of war were gathering my friend Phil Brown and I joined the Clyde division of the Royal Naval Volunteer Reserve in case war broke out, thus ensuring that when war was declared we would join the Navy. We were warned to stand by and were called up in the spring of 1940, drafted to *King Alfred* training establishment in Hove, Sussex and billeted in adjoining hotels and boarding houses. As far as I can remember we reported for duty in running shorts at 07.00 hours when we had to run from the *King Alfred* to Brighton Pier and back, then breakfast and home to change, wash and brush up. Classes started at 09.00 hours until lunch-time, and in the afternoon they recommenced and, with a short break for tea, continued until 19.00 hours and sometimes later. I know I never had the energy to 'go on the town' and just was glad to fall into bed. We had exams at the end of each week and it was hard work mastering each subject, for these included first aid, mine and bomb disposal, seamanship, navigation and chart correction, signalling with flags, morse code lights, gunnery, torpedoes, aircraft recognition, etc. . . . These were crash courses as the Admiralty were very short of officers, and in a month I was commissioned as a Lieutenant RNVR and posted to HMS *Clarkia* laying at Harland and Wolf's shipyard in Belfast. While at the *King Alfred* I shared a room with Lord Curzon and Whitehead, who later became managing director of Schweppes.

From 15th April, 1940 until the 9th May 1940 I served on HMS *Clarkia*, a Flower Class Corvette. Within a fortnight we had her stored, fuelled and ammunitioned, and sailed for Plymouth, where we worked her up, testing everything, speed, firing practice, etc. Those were days of hard work and little sleep but finally fully commissioned, we sailed as escort to a convoy proceeding north. While working up in the Channel we were strafed by a German plane and I got my first fire baptism. We fought the plane off without casualties. Whilst in Belfast we were adopted by the Women's League of Health and Beauty, who entertained us right royally!

Just as that time an AFO (Admiralty Fleet Order) came out stating that no RNVR officer over 35 years of age was to be allowed to go to sea in corvettes, this was a terrible blow and though my Captain tried in every way to retain me, I had to return to dry land, receiving an appointment to assist the Naval Officer in Charge at Thurso, Caithness, the end of the railway line, where one embarked for the Orkneys and Shetland Isles. I was very sorry as I thought this was the end of my seagoing.

HMS *Prosperpine* - NOIC Thurso — May 1940 - 31st March, 1941 Captain W. Newcombe, RN in charge

After a few days' leave I reported to Ormlie Lodge, a hotel opposite the station, which had been taken over by the Navy as Headquarters. It was manned by Captain Newcombe (who had a wooden leg, having lost it during the First World War); a Lieut.-Com., RNVR, a Liverpool stockbroker; a Paymaster Lieut., ex bank clerk; two lieutenants, 1 Sub/Lt and two Wren Officers, 4 Wren ratings to man the telephone exchange 24 hours a day, and a Royal Marine servant to NOIC Regulating, and an RN Petty Officer to look after passing ratings. Our function was to meet all trains and to give RN personnel orders which vessel they had to join, and see to their transport to Scapa Flow, where units of the Home Fleet were anchored, and vice versa, meet the two vessels bringing Naval personnel going on leave or to new appointments. We had to phone Glasgow and Edinburgh to arrange trains, additional carriages if required and programme them so that no delays occurred. All this had to be done in maximum secrecy, using codes which were changed almost every day. I enjoyed the work, improvising as we went along.

Firstly we had to build an air raid shelter in the spacious grounds for the staff. It was a hard slog digging a deep hole in the clay soil, then felling trees for beams and covering them with turf as camouflage. Fortunately we never had to use it for it was always full of water due to the excessive rainfull in those parts, and many mornings the water had turned to ice. While the Captain and his Wren officer occupied the heated first floor, we had cabins in an extension with no heat or hot water except the small jug of shaving water brought to us by the duty Wren; unfortunately their duties did not extend to warming our beds!

At 8 a.m. we received over the telephone from the Orkneys the number of officers and ratings coming over with their destinations, and we telephoned Railway HQ in Edinburgh and arranged the trains for that evening; having made out all travel warrants we awaited the arrival of one steamer from Lyness and one from Kirkwall. As soon as the coastguards phoned to say vessels had been sighted, we raced down to Scrabster (the port) boarded vessesls on arrival and took the officers in order of seniority for a meal in the two hotels. Their meals finished, we took them to the train and saw them off. This was interesting, for many personalities passed through our hands, such as Noel Coward, 'Tubby' Clayton, actors, and well-known footballers.

Icelandic trawlers came into Scrabster to obtain the current course down the East Coast through the minefields and often they brought in Norwegians they had picked up from open boats at sea who we had to interrogate in order to obtain any useful information they may have regarding enemy craft, etc. I will never forget one couple who were picked up half-way across the North Sea who had escaped in a kayak. They were husband and wife and one of the handsomest and nicest couples I have ever met. We adopted and rested them, feeding them up before passing them down the line. They were hoping to go to the USA; they must have had a lot of influence for not many months later I received a postcard from Florida, bearing a British stamp, to say they reached the USA.

One morning we had an urgent telephone call from the Admiralty warning us that important personages were coming the next day in a special train to proceed to Scapa Flow, and under no circumstances were we to mention this for security reasons. As they were important we borrowed a Rolls-Royce belonging to the local laird, Mr Pilkington. There had been a heavy fall of snow and gale-force winds during the night and when the morning broke it was sunny but terribly cold. We closed the station to all civilians as the train came in, and as I approached it I saw Winston Churchill standing at the window.

Lord Halifax got out of the train first, came up to me and asked, "Would I be responsible for the despatch boxes?" By this time NOIC arrived, but we were not allowed on the train and had to stand in the freezing snow. I explained to Lord Halifax that we had a Rolls-Royce for the Premier and several large cars besides. I got hold of a van, drove it on to the platform, and loaded the despatch boxes and luggage, with a Royal Marine to guard it. Just as everyone was ready to proceed, the PM decided he would have a bath and come down later. I discovered that Mrs Churchill and Lady Halifax were on the train, so we put them into a car, telling them to board the second minesweeper (which had arrived with its sister the previous night) where the chef from the *Rodney* had prepared lunch for them.

Our programme by this time was running late, thanks to the PM's clean habits! Eventually he emerged and we guided him to the line of cars headed by the Rolls, gleaming in the frosty sunshine. He took one look at it and the chauffeur holding the door open, then turned back, walked down the line, and got into the Royal Hotel car, much to the driver's amazement. Having one or two details to attend to, I followed later with the car full of despatch boxes and luggage. I parked alongside the minesweepers and went aboard to see the Captain, who asked when the PM was coming aboard. To my amazement the PM was nowhere to be seen. On my way to the quay however I had noticed that our duty drifter was alongside the escort destroyers, and when it returned the Master came to me and said, "The PM sends his compliments, and will Mrs Churchill and Lord and Lady Halifax join him on the destroyer?" This I duly organized and sailed the minesweepers back to Lyness, wondering what was going to happen to all that wonderful food I had seen aboard! I would not allow the minesweepers to sail until I received a signature from the Captain for the despatch boxes and luggage, which made me very unpopular. I returned to the base tired and frozen but happy after watching the destroyer sail away.

The next day was a real stinker, snowing heavily with a strong wind and big seas running. We received a telephone call from Lyness asking us to send the drifter out to meet the destroyers. So two of us boarded the drifter and sailed out of the harbour in a blinding snowstorm and lay waiting, hoping the destroyers would not run us down, as visibility was nil. We had not long to wait. Suddenly we heard a loud splash and a destroyer had dropped anchor practically alongside. We felt our way carefully until the destroyer loomed in sight and we heard the Captain shout that he was lowering a gangway for the PM and Mrs Churchill. The sea was running very high, so that at one moment it looked as it we would land on the destroyer's deck, and the next as if it would land on our small craft. We could not lash the gangway and just held the end, trying to keep it level. The PM judged it nicely and was the first across. Mrs Churchill then came across when there was about a six foot drop to our deck — the PM shouted, "Clem, jump!" and she did just that. We caught her in our arms, much to our relief. When we landed the PM said to us, "Lieutenants, thank you, I want you to know that you held in your arms today that which is most precious to me — even more than life itself."

I saw them on to the train and was standing frozen, waiting to give the signal for the train to depart, when I heard a loud tapping on the window and the PM was beckoning to me. I thought, 'My God, what has gone wrong now?' NOIC was standing near me and said, "You had better go in." Somewhat apprehensively I entered the carriage and the PM, after thanking me again, said, "Lieutenant, you have been doing the most of the hard work — you must be nearly frozen — drink this," and he handed me a very generous neat whisky; fortunately the windows were frosted up and the NOIC could not see me. I gulped it down, thanked the great man and staggered out, waving the train away. (The PM and Mrs Churchill had been seeing Lord and Lady Halifax off to take up his appointment as Britain's Ambassador to the USA.)

*   *   *

One night I was awakened by the duty Wren in the small hours, saying, "The duty officer at RAF Wick fighter base wanted to speak to you."

The caller said, "Iain, you are a member of the Silent Service, so please do a confidential job for me — get into a car and come along the Thurso-Wick road and pick up two Senior RAF officers and I will meet you outside our Officers' Mess." I sallied forth, in my pyjamas and Naval cap and greatcoat, took a car and stole quietly away. After several miles I came across an upturned car in a ditch and two pie-eyed Senior RAF officers, both well known, who had been to a private party. Their first remark was, "Thank God it is the Navy, they can keep their mouths shut." I took them aboard and stole quietly to the outside of the RAF base and delivered them to my friend, who told them to lie down in his car till they were past the guard. To this day I have not revealed who they were, as I had been sworn to secrecy. Regretfully, later one was lost in the desert and the other died in an air crash.

* * *

It was Christmas Eve and the leave boat was due to dock when a mine was sighted floating just outside Scrabster harbour entrance. I agreed with the Harbour-master that if he told NOIC, he would cancel the trains and send the ship back, so the lads would not be home for Christmas Day. So another officer and I went down to the harbour and saw the mine bobbing up and down by the entrance of the breakwater. We realized something had to be done, so we went into the pub where all the Icelandic trawler captains foregathered and put the case to them. We asked for a volunteer for our hazardous enterprise, which was to take us out towards the mine, lower a boat and row us out with a long rope, row round the mine (putting fishing net weights on the rope and joining the two ends in a noose slip knot) take it aboard the trawler, then slowly tow the mine out to see and sink it by rifle fire.

Unfortunately there was a very heavy sea running and just as we were nearing the trawler I saw to my horror the mine bob up with the rope caught on one of its horns. I just had time to yell to the Icelandic rowers to lie down in the bottom of the boat, doing so myself, when with a roar the mine went up, filling the boat with water and upsetting it. We were all wearing heavy clothing and duffle coats, and sea boots, so there was no question of swimming; as we bobbed up and down we clung to the boat until the trawler rescued us. We were not hurt but I noticed the funnel of the trawler and some of the superstructure had holes caused by the mine. Well, those brave Icelanders ferried us quickly ashore and would not let us drive back until several glasses of hot rum had been consumed.

Of course NOIC got to hear of our escapade and put us up before the Admiral Commanding the Orkneys and Shetland for a court martial as we had acted without his consent. Much to the NOIC's anger the reply was, "The two officers showed great initiative," and he highly commended us — and the sailors got home for Christmas, thanks to our prompt action. I knew then I would not be long on NOIC's staff and so it proved, for I was drafted shortly afterwards, due to ACOS inviting me over to his house in Orkneys for dinner. When I arrived at his front door, the butler who took my coat proved to be the butler of the Managing Director of the Anchor Line. During conversation at dinner I expressed a wish to go back to sea, and this was obviously taken up by Admiral Binnie, for I was soon appointed to HMS *King George V*, our newest battleship.

HMS *King George V* carrying the flag of C-in-C Home Fleet, Admiral Tovey

— From 1st April, 1941 — 8th December, 1941

This came as a shock to me, I mean no officer graduates from a corvette to be a watchkeeping officer on a battleship, so it shows that at that time they must have been scraping the barrel. Security on her was very strict for few people knew she existed and the Germans certainly did not, so she was never mentioned even to the seagulls, and for this I was grateful. When we went into action, the people at home did not know we were on board!

Usually one gets a spot of leave between appointments, but in this case I left Thurso the next day, my fellow officers were green with envy, and the NOIC was red with rage.

Normally when you change appointments, as you leave your Captain gives you a reference. I did not want to embarrass the NOIC so left without. The only reference I took with me was a cheery, "Don't get your feet wet," from my fellow officers, and lipstick marks from the darling Wrens!!!

Joining a battleship that carried the flag is like joining a luxury hotel. Everything is done for you; you have a Royal Marine batman who 'does' for you. You have hardly settled in your cabin when a writer comes from the Captain's office with a form you have to sign giving date of joining, your next of kin and religion. . . I used to have great fun by stating my religion as 'Christian', in no time he was back saying 'with respect, that this was not a religion and would I mind putting down C of E, RC, or Non-Conformist, etc.' The next thing is to visit the Wardroom, to be met by a sea of faces all looking at you. I was lucky again for the Commander stepped forward greeting me by my Christian name, for we had both been at the same school in Glasgow. From that moment I was accepted and 'pink gins' kept coming down the line.

The majority of the officers were RN and of course the RNVR and RNR officers are very often the butt of their jokes; it is fatal not to reply to them and take it lying down, for if you hit back good humouredly they respect you. For instance, they ask you why you joined the Navy. I would reply, "It is not often that a landlubber gets the opportunity of showing you how to run it." This sally ensures your popularity with them!!?

On the corvette we were four in the Wardroom, on the *KGV* I never counted them, but there must have been several hundred. Fortunately for me I was seconded to the C-in-C when sailing as Asst Intelligence Officer, and was soon sent on an Intelligence course at the Admiralty in London, principally to learn to decode German wireless messages which we had to break down. This I found intensely interesting and difficult until you get the knack and have the patience to plod on. In harbour or at anchor I was an officer on the watch and paced the deck. This was somewhat nerve-racking for when at anchor in Scapa Flow one is in charge of calling away all the ship's boats and liberty boats for the men and officers, also visitors' boats. In a short time, with the help of my Quartermaster (an old seadog) I got into the swing and like all things once you get the knack, it's easy. Not so when C-in-C held his dinners inviting Captains of vessels in Company, for at the appointed hour all these boats converged on the *KGV* and you had to call them alongside in order of seniority, so a telescope was essential to see the flag and the stripes on the passenger. Even in wartime procedure had to be maintained. I fear this gave me grey hairs.

Famous personages came over that gangway — Mountbatten, Admiral Vian, Prince Philip, and even King George VI who spent a weekend on board. It was quite an event; we all had to wear our best uniforms, white gloves and swords if you had one, if not you had to borrow one from an officer off watch. The quarter-deck over HM's cabin was marked off, and woe betide any sailor or officer who walked over it! The King came into the Mess and mixed with the officers before dinner. He was in his element chatting away and happily smiling and put us all at ease. What a nice man he was!!!

Periodically we would be called upon to escort a convoy or aircraft carrier past Iceland and Norway, then return and swing on a buoy at Scapa. While in Scapa I sat for my interpreter's exam in Italian. I passed my French and Italian but alas my exam papers for German went down with the *Hood*, for I had sat my exam aboard *Hood* on the day before she sailed on her fatal voyage. I remember her passing us as she headed for the open sea. It was a beautiful red sunset and the vessel was blood-red in the fading light. She looked magnificent and stately. An old seadog beside me said suddenly, "That is a bad omen, sir, I would not like to be aboard her." Little did we realize we would be following her out. The next day when we heard the terrible news; the whole ship's company was stunned. For we were a Chatham ship, like *Hood*, and that meant we were manned from the same base. The hunt was on, we sailed north, escorted by destroyers and joined the other vessels sweeping the seas — as you know, we caught up with the *Bismark*, and helped to sink her by gunfire.

I do not propose to go into details of the battle which has been extensively written about and even made into a film. Throughout the chase I took my share of running the Admiral's plot. This consisted of receiving all wireless signals on fleet movements and plotting them on the chart, so that C-in-C could see at a glance the position of his fleet. The weather was foul and we ran into heavy fog and lost her and we had to guess where she was running for, and it was on my watch that Admiral Tovey decided she would run to Brest. This proved right, and he brought his ship up accordingly to trap her. The whole operation was exceedingly exciting, particularly the last 24 hours.

We started preparations the day before the battle, so when we closed up for action stations the ship's chapel was turned into a casualty station. We all changed our underwear and dressed in white, to save getting blood poisoning if wounded. Large basins of disinfectant were placed in all alley-ways and doors taken down from cabins, and we lived on sandwiches, coffee, tea and cocoa for the next 24 hours. In all we were standing-to for nearly all that time. I remember that after the battle we foregathered for a drink in the mess and then crawled to our cabins; my feet were so swollen that I could not take my shoes off. I went to bed with my clothes and shoes on until I was wakened for my next watch, and by that time the swelling had subsided and I was able to change.

Just before opening fire we closed all watertight doors and I was sent down to the lower communication centre with all my secret code books. Should we have been hit I would not have been able to get out. In fact just before the battle, the *Bismark* sent out coded messages which I decoded, calling for air cover, which of course never came. . . When she went down I did not hear a cheer, we were all so half-stunned and tired. For all our guns were firing at once (we had ten 14.5-inch guns and eight 5.25-inch) the noise and vibration was tremendous. The only casualty we had was the Royal Marine guarding the keyboard flat, which was right under the after guns; poor chap, he did not desert his post and was bounced up against the bulkhead until he became unconscious. I am glad to say he recovered and got a special mention.

After the battle we limped to the nearest fuelling station in the west of Scotland and just made it before running out of fuel. Then we proceeded to Scapa Flow and Rosyth to have our engines and guns checked and restored and re-ammunitioned. We were all very glad of the rest.

Admiralty sent a signal to C-in-C and the Captain congratulating them and asked them to submit names for decorations. Captain Paterson replied 'No damage, no casualties, no medals'. Nevertheless the Captain, Guns and Chief Engineer received DSOs and they richly deserved them.

When we returned to Scapa Flow I was appointed to XDO Kirkwall, on 8th December, 1941. I dined with C-in-C Home Fleet the night before I left; I was at that time the only RNVR officer he had dined. The custom was that he sent his Flag Officer to advise you and on the night you met for drinks in his quarters, after which you adjourned to his dining-room where at your place you found a printed card bearing the C-in-C's flag and your name; dinner finished the port went round — the most junior officer present raised his glass and proposed the toast to His Majesty the King, after which we adjourned to the Wardroom for the cinema, and that finished we all stood at attention while C-in-C left. As he passed me he asked me to follow. When I got to Tovey's quarters I found myself alone with him and he asked me to sit down. His steward asked me what I would like to drink and as we had had quite a few drinks that night I asked for a beer. Tovey said, "Nonsense, you are a Scot," and ordered me a large malt whisky, after which he said, "I am led to believe you have a good repertoire of Commercial Travellers' stories." (Hence the large whisky.) I kept him laughing for some time and I could see him unwind and the tension disappear. He said if ever my ship was in Company I was to make myself known. Alas we never met again, for I left the ship early next morning.

HMS *Pyramus*
XDO (Extended Defence Officer) Kirkwall, Orkneys.
Captain E. Hoyle in command.   From 8th December, 1941
to 15th February, 1942.

I was stationed at Rewick Head, a bleak and lonely spot where we had a look-out tower built overlooking the Pentland Firth, from which the minefield was controlled. We kept sea watches as on a ship. The work was not difficult but tiring as one had to concentrate on all shipping passing in and out of Kirkwall. The minefield laid was a magnetic one, so when any iron or steel vessel passed over it there was a swing registered. This was principally laid to stop enemy submarines sneaking in. When the swing took place you had to decide whether to pull the lever which activated the mines and blew up whatever was passing at the time. It had to be done in seconds so you had no time before making the decision. The weather was very severe, the winds were so strong that it took me half an hour to cover about 100 yards mostly on hands and knees, for if you stood up you were blown off your feet; I was glad to reach the tower and warmth and shelter. Captain Hoyle was a very charming gentleman and a pleasure to take his orders. Unfortunately there was little to do between watches and a lot of drinking took place. My early training stood me in good stead, i.e. no drinking for four hours before coming on watch. Though on all my other flimsies there is no reference to drink, Captain Hoyle states on his that I conducted myself with sobriety! We had no transport and had to rely on the army for a lift into Kirkwall, where there was little to do except eat and drink in the hotel. Strangely, so many years later, I rowed on the Thames and pulled into a small island for tea, and who should be the manageress of the hotel but the couple who ran the Kirkwall Hotel!

I think I was given this appointment to give me a rest and restore my equilibrium.

HMS *Despatch* Light Cruiser
Commander in Command — Maurice Huntington-Whiteley
Captain — W. Leggat
8th April, 1942 to 25th September, 1943

I joined this ship at Chatham, where she was refitting after a commission in the West Indies, and was intending to return there on being recommissioned. Our home at that time was with friends in Ashford, Kent, which was very convenient for I could get home at weekends. The weather was beautiful and a pleasant change from the weather of the Orkneys.

Eventually we were ready for sea and fully recommissioned, completed trials, and sailed for Gibraltar with our new Captain Leggat, RN (a very tall handsome man). He had been British Naval Attaché in Turkey and other diplomatic posts. Whenever we left port he would be seasick for the first days. On reaching Gibraltar we received orders to sail for Freetown for convoy duties on the West African coast. We were disappointed, for the chance of seeing any action was remote. On the other hand out of all the officers on board, there were only three of us, including myself, who had seen a shot fired in anger — (the Warrant Engineer and Guns). Fortunately we saw quite a lot of sea time escorting convoys bound for Pointe-Noire to fuel and saw them safely round the Cape, always coming back to Freetown, the only place we were allowed to go ashore. Apart from my watchkeeping duties I was Wardroom Wine Officer and Ship's Sports Officer, organizing football matches with ships in company and shore bases. I would take my teams on night route marches finishing at Lumley Beach for a swim at dawn. Incidentally, we had the best health record on the African coast.

While on the station we were ordered to proceed to the Cape Verde Islands and intercept a Spanish flag vessel the *Monte Naranco* making her way to Spain from the Plate, with alleged contraband on board. We sailed as soon as all the crew were aboard. Just as we sighted the Islands we saw the ship, an old coalburner. We signalled her to stand-by for a boarding party. I was appointed boarding officer and had to pick my team of twelve; much to the Captain's surprise I picked the worst rascals, some of whom had served gaol sentences. They were led by a huge red-headed leading hand from Birmingham, who had a lion tattooed on his chest. He was very hairy and trimmed it so that the lion had a mane and a tuft on its tail!

We loaded gear and provisions on our motor boat and went alongside. The steamer's crew threw us a rope ladder and I had to be the first to climb up. Have you ever tried climbing a rope ladder with a heavy haversack and a .45 naval revolver in your hand? Somehow I struggled aboard with the Spaniards giving me a hand (all against regulations). I explained to the Captain that we had orders to take him to Gibraltar for examination; fortunately he was an old seadog and spoke fluent English. I had a sparks (electrician) with me who took over their W/T. I took over the bridge with a Lieutenant, who was leading so that we could keep alternate watches. I saw on deck earthenware jars that periodically the stokers came up and took a drink from and to my horror I found they contained wine which the crew gallantly offered to my sailors. I made a quick decision, called my crew together, and promised them that if they obeyed orders not to touch liquor while on board, I would see to it that they would not be crimed in Gibraltar if they were drunk. Much to my amazement they obeyed the rule. The vessel was carrying some tinned fruit in her cargo and soldered inside we would find platinum, which was urgently required by the Germans. Secondly, among the crew were three members of the *Graf Spee* trying to get back to Germany. They had forged papers and spoke fluent Spanish. I interrogated the whole crew who were all equally sunburnt, and hair bleached by the sun; we had to discover who were the Germans before reaching Gibraltar or our names would be mud! I thought over this problem again and again then I hit on an idea.

Next morning I cleared lower decks and when they were all assembled I went below and searched through the crew's clothing. Problem solved, for the three who had the cleanest shirts and underwear were the Germans. They admitted it later but we had them safely locked up and handed over to the Military Police in Gibraltar.

The next problem was to rejoin our ship. Life was very monotonous. We only had our crew to look after and they behaved themselves, in fact we were complimented for our discipline and smartness. I shared a room with a much decorated Flight Lieutenant, who had been sent to Gibraltar for a rest. He was as nervous as a kitten and would jump out of bed in the middle of the night and start pacing up and down. He would apologize to me profusely in the morning and just could not believe that I could fall asleep two minutes after being wakened. I showed him how to relax and by the end of a week he was sleeping soundly.

After about ten days HMS *Despatch* called to pick us up and stores, and take on some Nissen huts for a secret destination. After 24 hours at sea the Captain revealed we were sailing for Brazil, where we were to take our refit.

I will never forget crossing the South Atlantic — balmy nights with brilliant moon, twinkling stars, and also fantastic electrical storms including St Elmo's lights, for this is when the atmosphere is so charged with static electricity that the ship's rigging lights up like neon lighting, so that the whole ship looked like a Christmas tree; a fantastic sight. Beautiful but dangerous for we would have been a sitting target for a submarine. Happily all went well and with great relief we sighted the South American coastline, making a landfall at Recife where we refuelled and learned with joy that we were going to have a refit. It was wonderful to have lights on at night and not to have to go about stumbling on your way to take over your watch on the bridge.

On the way to Rio we called in at Bahia, a very colourful place. Boats filled with all kinds of tropical fruit surrounded the vessel. While I was on watch on the quarter deck one evening, a young Captain of the Brazilian Army asked permission to come on board and look round. His name was de Fonsecca-Hermes. He spoke excellent English and we invited him for dinner next day. He turned out to be the son of the former President of Brazil and he gave me a written introduction to his parents in Rio. Later that week we sailed for Rio and our dream sequence continued. Calm seas and moonlit nights. Then early one morning we all marvelled at the beauty of the entrance to Rio dominated by the Corcovada mountain with its gigantic statue of Jesus at the top. Skirting Nikteroi Island we berthed alongside the main square opposite the NOITE Newspaper building in the middle of the town; it was staggering.

We were soon boarded by Embassy and Consular officials and members of the British Colony coming aboard to adopt our sailors and officers. I remember I had the middle watch, so did not join in the festivities that night. Next day the watches were altered so that we had 24 hours off and 24 hours on, this allowed the crew greater liberty. The hospitality was out of this world. If you went into a bar and ordered a drink, when it was put before you a Brazilian got up and toasted your health — that meant he was paying for the drink, then if you ordered another drink or tried to return a drink, up would pop another Brazilian and toast "President Vargas", so you never paid for a drink; this seems to have applied to the crew as well. I must say the Colony had a wonderful organization watching over our boys right through the night, so there were no civic disturbances or fights. There was a bar in the square opposite our berth and one old Leading Hand, our 'Chippy', never got further than that bar the whole time we were in Rio.

I contacted the Fonsecca-Hermes, who entertained me in their palatial home. After dinner he took me down to his strong room, which was like a bank vault. There I saw a whole wall of shelves with leather bound stamp albums with his family crest emblazoned in gold; he took a couple down and showed me that on the pages his wife had painted the flag and shield and name of the country, with flowers of that country down all the edges. . . truly a labour of love over many years. He told me he had the third largest and most valuable collection in the world, and I believed it.

After our dry-docking, repairs and storing were over and it was time to leave, we threw a dance on board and our Royal Marines beat the retreat; the Brazilians loved it and it was a fitting end to a very memorable visit. I was also entertained by an official of the Cable and Wireless and his wife and family. His teenage daughter and son took me out sailing in their yacht. The boy told me he was joining the British Navy to train as a submariner. Little did I know our paths would cross in Italy at Tarranto, where we had a one man submarine base. He went on a most perilous trip and lost his life, for which he was awarded the Victoria Cross posthumously.

On our return to West Africa via Gibraltar, we sailed for Dakar to seize the port and the French vessels lying there, among which was a French battleship, *Jean Bart*. The Navy had tried to seize it before but were repulsed with some losses, however, Intelligence told us they were now ready to surrender. So we sailed in, escorted by destroyers, and were happy to see our Intelligence was correct, for their ship guns were not at the ready. The surrender took place aboard our ship and I acted as interpreter, aided by a fellow RN officer. The talks were successful and in no time I was organizing soccer and Rugby matches, and boxing between the British and the French Navy.

After the Rugby match I was asked to make a speech, so I invited them aboard for a party the next day. There was some doubt as to whether they would come as, up to then, while being frigidly polite, they had not let themselves go. We need not have had any fears for they all turned up with their wives and children, grandparents as well. The sailors quickly turned our capstan into a roundabout, organized races for the kids, and some of our sailors made perfect clowns and laughter was everywhere.

We were there about ten days and left as soon as the surrender was completed. The French were amazed that we walked ashore without firearms and that we were ready to extend a hand in friendship. The civil governor of French Equatorial Africa was not prepared to be friendly and at the talks was very hostile. However, he met his Waterloo, for when the last rounds of talks were completed and the surrender signed, we served champagne and at the toast "Vive la France" we all stood up, and the trousers of the Civil Governor fell down! Such is Naval discipline, no one smiled or laughed and we carried on with drinking the toast quickly so that we could all sit down and allow the Civil Governor to recover what dignity he had left.

I do not know how long we were supposed to stay in Dakar but our visit was cut short by orders to sail and patrol the coast, as the *Queen Mary* loaded with troops was expected to pass on her way to the East, and a German raider had been sighted. We met the *Queen* and escorted her as far as we could at full speed, about 25 knots, but we soon had to sail into Pointe-Noire to refuel and had no hope of catching her up.

We sailed out of Pointe-Noire to escort a convoy round the Cape of Good Hope, and as we were reaching the Cape a fierce gale broke out and we ploughed through it. I remember we were heading right into it. Our bridge was awash and it was 35 ft above sea level. Our forward gun turret was taking a frightful pasting. Then we received a signal from the destroyers asking us "for God's sake slow down," which we did, much to our relief, for I was soaked through and afraid the gun turret might find itself overboard. We went on after rounding the Cape, leaving the convoy off Madagascar and returned slowly to the Naval base of Simonstown. When we reached Simonstown and dry-docked, we found the foredeck and gun turret had dropped two feet, so we had a pleasant rest and were all adopted by various families. I was adopted by an ex-British jockey, now training horses for Garlick, the big store owner. They lived outside Cape Town in a lovely villa and looked after me, spoiling me completely. They had a young daughter who was engaged, and a son, a midshipman, who was lost at sea. One day they proudly showed me a photograph of him and here fate gave me another blow — he had been my midshipman of the watch on *King George V* and, not liking being on a big ship, had wanted to sail in a destroyer. I mentioned it to the Captain, who said he would try and arrange it. Shortly afterwards he was appointed to a Tribal Class Destroyer, I think it was the *Ashanti*. The very next time the *KGV* went out escorted by destroyers, one of them got a ping on a submarine and shot across *KGV's* bows. Unfortunately they must have miscalculated our speed and we hit her amidships, turned her completely over, and we heard the crunching noise as our keel passed over her. It was the *Ashanti*, she never surfaced again and my midshipman went down with her. I told his parents the full story and strange to say they were glad to hear how their son had died and to meet a person who was pretty well the last to see him, and we became great friends. I was able to do something for them for the daughter was getting married, and with special permission from my Captain, I was able to supply all her bed linen, towels, etc., of first-class British make which it was impossible to find in South Africa at that time.

Another vivid memory was a game of Rugby we played against the South African Navy. It was very rough and I received a kick in the head, giving me concussion. I awoke with my head on a very pretty S. African Wren's lap. The next day I was asked to a party at their quarters for 8 p.m. By that time it was pitch dark and as I made my way up the hill and neared their quarters, I heard an exclamation and received a quivering assegai at my feet! Believe me I stopped dead in my tracks and the next moment a huge native appeared wanting to know my business. He escorted me to the Wrenery and stood there till I was claimed. The girls were certainly well guarded.

When the vessel was ready we sailed and escorted a convoy up to Freetown, where later we received the joyful news that we were to sail for home and pay-off, finishing our commission. Berthing at Chatham, flying our pay-off pennant, we all had a load of 'rabbits' to take home and my sailors asked me how they could get them past the Customs. As Officer-in-Charge of Wines the Custom Officers looked through my books and found them in order. I noticed they hesitated, and when their senior officer left to see the Captain they asked me if they could buy a bottle each of whisky and Drambuie.

I replied, "Why not have a case each?" They looked at me unbelievingly and asked how they could get it ashore without being seen.

"Leave it to my sailors and I will arrange to have the middle watch," I said. "If you come quietly alongside I will arrange to have sailors place four cases in your launch and they will unload them at the railway wharf." (This was outside the Customs' barrier.) They readily agreed.

So the next night I got four cases on the deck next to the gangway and told my men to collect all their 'rabbits' and hide them on the other side of the deck, and when the launch came alongside to rush down with their cases, then make a chain on the gangway and pass the four cases of liquor down to the Customs launch. The two most trusted ratings went to discharge the launch at the station, where they had to wake up the staff, and put their cases, including mine in the left luggage, handing the tickets for the officers' cases to the officers, and I sent a boat ashore for them later. The operation went like a dream: mind you, the Customs officers were hopping mad, but what was sauce for the goose was also sauce for the gander! So my men did not have to pay a penny duty, much to the amazement of the rest of the crew — after all I was only obeying the unwritten law that a Naval officer must at all times look after the interests of his men. They were a fine loyal bunch and deserved being looked after.

So we were all paid-off and went on leave, laden with silk stockings, bunches of bananas, sacks of sugar, tobacco, cigarettes and booze. The night before we officially dispersed we took a box at the local music hall where Billy Bennett 'almost a gentleman' was appearing. I went round the back and took him a bunch of bananas and he ended his act by saying, "I am now going to perform a trick nobody else can perform in Britain today," and he hauled out of his baggy trousers a banana, which he proceeded to peel and eat to the howls of laughter from the audience.

I felt very sad for I had grown to love my ship, my men, and the adventures we had shared, without a single casualty.

Thus ended my sea appointments, much to my sorrow, for it was on HMS *Despatch* that I earned my Watchkeeping Certificate.

Taranto — 15th November, 1943

After a few months ashore, which entailed undergoing Intelligence and Security courses at Admiralty, Matlock, I was appointed as Fleet Base Security Officer in Taranto, Adriatic and Lower Italy. I took up this appointment on 15th November, landing shortly after Taranto's liberation from a fast minesweeper, the *Ariade*, which I had boarded at Portsmouth. The *Ariade* carried in her mine-holds Christmas mail for the ships in the Mediterranean Fleet, and when I joined for passage the First Lieutenant, a 2½-ringer, RN, asked me if I would take a watch to which I readily agreed. I was given the middle watch, 12-4 a.m., and the next night it was the same. One night during the voyage the Captain came up on the bridge and asked me who had requested that I take the watch, as I was supposed to be a passenger, and he quizzed me how long and what watches I had kept. He sent for the Number One on the bridge and gave him what in the Navy is called 'tearing off a strip', so my watches ended, for which I was sorry, as the vessel was lovely to handle, doing speeds of well over 30 knots not full out. We called at Gibraltar, Algiers, Malta, where we were bombed but no hits, but their mail was discharged double quick time and we were soon on our way again, arriving safely at Taranto.

I reported to Admiral McGrigor who gave me a lovely office overlooking the harbour. I was lucky, for being one of the first to land I managed to get a cabin overlooking the Mar Piccolo sea, and anchored under my window was the Italian training ship *Amerigo Vespucci*, a 3-masted long ship. In Taranto I acted mainly as liaison officer between the Admiral and the Italian Navy, so was in at all the meetings as an interpreter. I shall never forget one meeting when our Admiral sent for the Italian Admiral of the dockyard to ask him politely, "Would he undertake the repairs of the Royal Navy vessesls?" Admiral Correali, the Italian Admiral, got up and made a long speech making excuses of every kind. Our Admiral was looking anxious by this time so when the Admiral paused for breath I got up and said, "Admiral Correali said 'yes'." The laughter came from both sides and friendly relations were established. The work was interesting but a bit nerve-racking as I was in charge of security from Naples round the toe of Italy to Bari, a very large coastline area. I managed to get a jeep from the Americans to cover distances and fortunately the locals were only too glad to point out where the retiring German and Italian army had mined the various posts, so I went up and down the coast marking the maps and we never had a casualty. The Italian fishermen had certainly kept their eyes open. I compensated them by giving those individuals permission to fish in certain areas (although all fishing was officially prohibited).

I found a lovely flat which I commandeered. It had the finest bathroom in Taranto and a telephone! I used it to interview informers who were afraid to come to Naval Headquarters. There was plenty of hot water and the plumbing worked!

The Germans had either drunk all the wine or carried it away. The RN Roman Catholic Padre came to me and asked me if I would accompany him to a monastery in the hills, which had some very fine wines. The Padre spoke no Italian and had been thinking he could converse in Lation as he had learned Latin at Oxford, but they could not understand him! I could not believe it and went up in a lorry and sure enough the Abbot said he could not understand the Priest but when I explained we were willing to pay for the wine, we came back with a lorry load but kept it dark! So I was never short of good wine. The good Abbot thought we were like the Germans and would seize the wine without paying.

The work was very arduous but I had one great satisfaction, for during my appointment there we did not have a single act of sabotage, although we had to shoot a young Italian for stabbing and killing a soldier outside a tavern.

Rome

I became friendly with the Italian Naval Liaison Officer, Lieut. Rossi, who had his family in Rome, which was still in German occupation. I promised I would arrange to take him there as soon as the city was liberated. I was glad to be able to do this; we loaded a jeep full of stores and set out carrying our revolvers with us, as many people were waylaid by American Army deserters. On the way my Italian Franco Rossi told me he had had no word of his family since the Germans occupied Italy, and that his uncle was a Cardinal in the Vatican. It was a most emotional meeting. We drove up to the apartment building, I let him go up first but could hear their cries as I followed.

They were speechless and all weeping tears of joy. Thank God he found them all well but looking thin. We soon put that to rights when we unloaded our car. They said if it had not been for their uncle in the Vatican giving them some food, they would have starved, for the Germans took all the food in the shops.

Vatican visit — Presented to Pope

I visited the Vatican as a guest of Cardinal Rossi and lunched with him, after which he took me through to the library where I met the Pope, who insisted that I sat down. He asked my name and when I said I was a Scot, he said, "All Scots are good Christians and attend church regularly." We had quite a chat and he put me at ease right away. He instructed the Cardinal to give me a relic, which was a gold locket containing a lock of a Saint's hair, with a signed parchment as to its authenticity. (When I reached home I gave it to my sister-in-law, who was a convert to Roman Catholicism, and a teacher at Brompton Oratory, where the nuns weened it away, so I never got it back, although to me it was just a souvenir.)

Trieste

Very suddenly I received orders to pack my bags and to proceed to the airport, where a Hurricane fighter plane was waiting to fly me to Ancona, as news denoted that Trieste would be freed at any moment. We touched down safely and I was met by a jeep and taken into the town where a port party was waiting in two jeeps to proceed with the New Zealand Division and General Freyburg, VC, to liberate Trieste. Next morning we proceeded on the coast road behind the NZ tanks. The weather was hot and the fumes from the tanks nearly choked us, so we decided to worm our way to the front. Finally we got through and belted ahead, and rounding a corner met a German naval lieutenant coming towards us waving a white sheet, followed by his ratings. We handed them over to the first NZ tank and proceeded with a warning from the Germans that the Yugoslavs were advancing and had reached the outskirts of Trieste. As we had some urgent jobs to do, we hurried on, soon to be shot at by our gallant allies. However, we arrived safely at the Hotel Corso, where we were to make our naval Mess.

The streets were rapidly filling with jubilant Italians, mostly girls, covering us with flowers and singing. When the NZ tanks arrived they had soldiers hugging girls on top. By this time the Yugoslavs had ceased firing and marched in. We posted all our armed ratings at the entrance to the banks before the Yugoslavs got there. However, we need not have worried for the Yugoslavs were too busy raiding the shops, which were empty — the Germans had seen to that.

That night I was out all night contacting the various Italian and Yugoslav authorities and arranging for the safety of the harbour which we knew was mined. But the retreating Germans were persuaded by the Italian Port Authorities not to set them off. My next job was to locate and remove these mines. Fortunately after blowing open a safe at what had been the German HQ, I found a map with all the mine placings marked.

Our naval contingent consisted of a Capt. RN, a Commander RN, a Royal Marine Provo Marshall and several technical officers to take over the town and I was glad when they arrived, for I had little sleep as I was the only Italian-speaking member until then. By this time I had learned a lot from my Taranto appointment and in no time things were falling into place. Our Commander was one of the Guinness family and straight away arranged for a meeting to be held every morning at 7 a.m. to discuss the day's work, and another at 6 p.m. to discuss what had been arranged or completed. He was a hard task master but fair and saw to it that there was no slacking.

We soon had the port clear of mines and the ships could come in with stores, etc., for up to then we were severely rationed. Here again I got the fishing organized and we had regular supplies for our Mess. I had to ration the permits to fish, for some would sail to trade their fish if they could get a better price, but they were a security risk.

All this time I was collecting intelligence for my superiors in London. Then to complicate matters, the American Navy arrived and wanted me to share my intelligence with them, which I could not do, as their standards of secrecy left a lot to be desired. But that is another story.

War Booty Officer

Just as my group was coming up for demobilization, I was appointed War Booty Officer. This work entailed raking through the docks, shipyards, factories, etc., with the Yugoslavs and making a list of all kinds of stores, machinery, cars, electrical gear, arms, mines, torpedoes, etc., and tracing their origin, so that at a weekly meeting we could decide whether the article should be declared War Booty of the Italians or Yugoslavs. This was quite a headache as the Yugoslav Generals claimed everything they could lay their hands on, irrespective of origin. They had an interpreter who spoke excellent English and was a Communist. I decided we could not accept his interpretations as no one on our side understood Yugoslav, which in itself contained more than one language, i.e. Slovene, Albanian, Croat, Yugoslav, etc. I was also highly suspicious of some of the whisperings and asides which sounded like Russian. Eventually, through my grapevine, it was proved that of the seven Generals four were indeed Russian in Yugoslav uniform. I decided to challenge them by saying Russians were our Allies too and if the Yugoslavs insisted bringing the Russians in, we would bring the Americans, Poles, and French in to decide. The meeting broke up and at the next meeting we had some new faces.

This work entailed travelling all over North Italy where the Germans had left countless barges which were claimed as War Booty. These barges had been transported, some of them cut in half, as this was done by rail and road, often the two not arriving at the same time, so some barges had German bows and Dutch sterns, with the Yugoslavs claiming the one and the Dutch the other. We were also hampered by the Italians who tried to spirit some away along the coast and up the River Po. We got a list of the missing barges from Allied HQ and by the time I left Trieste to be finally demobbed most of the barges had been accounted for, but of course some had been lost in action. One of the most interesting items we traced were six torpedoes built by the Austrians before the First World War and carefully 'moth-balled' and hidden in a cave just outside Pola harbour. Experts from the Admiralty came over to look at them and the most amazing thing I heard later was that they were tested and their motors went off first shot. These were never produced as War

Booty but smuggled to the UK to be placed in a War Museum.

Thus I packed my bags and returned to the UK by rail via Austria, to see my long suffering wife and meet my daughter who did not recognize me and took umbrage at my getting into bed with her mother.

* * *

If I were asked what, if any, benefits I received from my service with the Navy in wartime, I would reply — firstly the pride in the work I was doing and secondly, love of my country and its ships; then how to control my fear so that it was not communicated to my men, also the more senior the Royal Navy officer, the nicer they are, and lastly the loyalty of the seamen to their ship and officers.

During the whole time I was at sea my men never let me down and they never took advantage of my ignorance of RN customs or procedure, so thereby I never received a red face; that danger is a great leveller.

Would that in peacetime men had the same ideals of unselfishness, service and love of their country.

* * *

VARIOUS VIGNETTES

There is no time, date and sometimes places in the following jottings which are put down as I remember them.

Taranto

During my period there I was asked by the Italian Admiral could I teach English to some of his junior officers. As our Admiral had approved this approach I thought I had better comply, so I arranged two classes a week. I started by teaching them the English equivalents of sailing ships and their sails, then went on to parts of a warship, guns, etc. . . . All went very well until one very hot afternoon when my young pupils showed signs of nodding off. I said jokingly, "Instead of dressing a ship, let us undress a woman," teaching the English for the various garments. They jolly soon woke up and showed great interest and of course I had my back to the door. Suddenly I heard my class jump to their feet and on looking over my shoulder I saw the two Admirals at the door. How long they had been there I did not know. All I knew was that the Italian Admiral dismissed the class with baleful looks at me and they all walked out. Next morning our Admiral sent for me. I made a clean breast of it (although we had not gone as far as that part) telling him my reason for digressing to keep the class awake. He laughed heartily, but the class was discontinued.

As our relations with the Italian naval fraternity were very cordial, our

Admiral threw a cocktail party inviting all senior Italian officers, among which was the Italian submarine ace who had placed the charge under the Admiral's ship. He was a very handsome young man with auburn hair and a Marchese to boot. His wife, who was very beautiful, was also invited but the Marchese was insanely jealous, so when she went to the w.c. before leaving for the party the Marchese locked her in, taking the key with him, and apologizing for her absence saying she was not well. Some time later our Admiral invited them for dinner. La Marchesa said to her husband that it would be nice to take one of her famous cream cakes. When the Marchese was dolled up with full decorations and ready to leave, his wife fetched the cream cake and while he was looking at it, she spilled it all over him and he had to phone and cancel their visit!

Trieste

My appointment included security of the Port of Pola (now called Pula under Yugoslavia). I had to make periodical visits and as the intervening territory was occupied by Yugoslav troops, I had permission to use the main road, providing I did not stop on the journey.

Half-way I discovered a lovely inn which decanted some excellent white wine from their own vineyard. It was very hot on these trips and despite the risk I ran, I used to stop, once on the way down and once on the way up. The innkeeper became quite friendly as I used to do the trip once a month. Pola has always been famous for its lobsters, and on one of these trips 'Flags' asked me to get six for the Admiral. Well on the way back I did not have a box, so they were crawling everywhere and I could not concentrate on my driving, so I stopped at the inn to have a drink of Mine Host's delectable ice-cold 'yellow gold' and to borrow a box. I went in, placing the lobsters on the floor, and ordered my drink, with my back to the entrance. As I watched him pour out a glass, I suddenly saw him go pale and his hand started to shake.

I knew instantly it must be the Yugoslav soldiery and so it was, two of them, pointing their guns at me and, I presume, calling in Slovene for me to put my hands up. Instead I ordered a bottle of wine in Italian for the soldiers and reaching for my glass raised it, giving a toast to our gallant Allies the Yugoslav Army. Fortunately one of the soldiers spoke Italian. They were nonplussed but still held me covered. I explained I had been asked by the Yugoslav Captain of the port to take the lobsters as a gift to our Admiral and unless you keep lobsters moving they get tough, so I stopped here and the Landlord kindly permitted me to exercise the lobsters and have a drink, as the day was very hot. I asked them to join me. They did so gladly, and I saw the relief on the innkeeper's face. It was a close call, not that they would have shot me, but they would have forced me to be taken to prison for questioning, and I would have languished there until they thought fit or enquiries were made as to my disappearance, which might have taken days or weeks. As an Intelligence officer I would have never lived it down, and the lobsters would have ended up in some foreign stomach! Fortunately I was not carrying a gun! Therefore I had to keep a cool head, as the Yugoslavs are rather trigger-happy.

My thoughts were also for the innkeeper, who might have been tried and shot. When they accepted a drink I knew they would not report the event. The lobsters certainly avoided an international incident!!!

The RN Harbour-master was a great character — as mad as a hatter (George Cross and Bar) and had hollow legs, he always carried a gerbal tucked in his shirt and exercised it along the bar counters of every bar in Trieste. One day we met up with an American officer who challenged us to go down some steep steps in our jeep. We performed this exercise without any trouble, whereupon he tried, but came a terrible cropper, smashing up his jeep.

One evening as I was walking up a street I heard a terrific noise coming from a bar. I went over to see one our seamen in a corner being attacked by 6 American soldiers; he already had three of them laid on the floor. I rushed to a phone and spoke to the Provo-Marshal, by the time his men got there the sailor had knocked another one down and the remainder had run away.

When he appeared for Captain's defaults, I pleaded self-defence and he got off despite American prosecution.

I was having a swim in a bay near Trieste when an Italian, who had been doing high diving, came up and said there was something like a shark near the bottom, but it was bigger and not moving. So I dived and swam to the bottom and saw that it was an Italian one man submarine. I took another dive to make sure, and when I rose to the surface felt a terrible pain in my ears and found they were bleeding. However, I managed to clear the beach of bathers, phoned from the nearest phone, and raced back to Trieste, putting the place out of bounds. Next day I went with the Salvage Officer and proper equipment, a barge with a crane, and raised the sub to the surface. It was full of water but the torpedo had been primed and was already for firing. Luckily the sea was calm, for a sudden knock or jerk would have set the torpedo off. Thank goodness the sailors handled the whole thing gingerly and we rendered the torpedo safe.

London

During one of my short leaves I stayed at the Regent Palace Hotel in Piccadilly Circus. Before dinner I went to the bar downstairs. Just as I was about to leave the crew of a submarine rushed in, officers and ratings, blocking the entrances, and a young Lieut. RN announced they had had a successful patrol and nobody would be allowed to leave until he or she had performed their party piece.

It was great fun, some were great sports, others objected strongly, but if they wanted to leave they were stopped. It was a wonderful cabaret watching the various performers. I remember a big fat lady getting on to a table, pulling up her skirts and doing a very creditable 'Can-can' and her escort telling very spicy jokes. I missed my dinner that night. I gave a rendering of 'Sandy McCluskey', which got quite a cheer.

HMS *King George V*

There was a young Royal Marine from Glasgow serving aboard, handsome, redheaded and tough. He had his birthday when we were at sea. The RMs on his messdeck had been saving up their rum rations for this event (which is contrary to KR & AI but nevertheless a custom on the lower deck). Well, they had the party and got the boy drunk; true to pattern he became fighting drunk and stabbed one of his mates with his bayonet, not seriously, but for the offence, being a serious one, he was clapped in irons and placed in the cells until we got to port. There he would be tried and sentenced to a long period in the glasshouse, and discharged the service with disgrace. The Major of RMs came to my cabin, saying how very upset the boy was and what a good soldier he had been. Knowing I had lived in Glasgow he asked me to go to the cells and have a word with him. I went down asking to be allowed to see him alone. The poor laddie was in a terrible state; realizing what he had done when drunk he broke down and cried, saying it would break his mother's heart, and begged me to help him. Firstly I saw the RM he had stabbed, who begged me to help the boy, as he had forgiven him. I knew his superior officer could not intervene, so I went to see our Captain, RN (Captain Paterson, who was also redheaded) telling him that I was sure he would never have any further trouble, if we could save the boy from prison, something which would ruin his career. He would have to become teetotal, and if I could obtain his promise never to touch alchohol until the war was over, could he just stop his leave ashore for the rest of the Commission? Well, I did obtain the boy's promise and the Captain agreed my terms. I heard that at the invasion of France he won the Military Medal for Valour.

While serving on HMS *King George V* I was allotted a Royal Marine batman, a smart, pleasant HO, who did my dobeying and kept my cabin clean. While in Scapa Flow he was due for leave and left for his home in Plymouth, but I was very surprised to see him back shortly after and shocked at his grim expression. He went about his work without a word. I saw his CO at dinner and questioned him. Apparently the boy's home was on the same street as his parents, his brother and his in-laws. Plymouth had received a severe strafing from enemy aircraft, and when he turned the corner into his street there was just a pile of ruins, and no survivors, so he just returned to his ship and sat in his messdeck staring in front of him, without speaking. His CO was very understanding when I suggested that he be allowed to stay in my cabin when I was on duty. I had plenty of books and magazines and a wireless. At the end of the week he had got over the shock and had a good cry, so he told me. He thanked me and wanted to repay me in some way. I said, "You can stand me a drink if we ever meet when this is all over."

About three years after the war when I was working in the City, I boarded a bus at Liverpool Street Station, sat down and tendered my fare without looking up, when I heard a voice say, "I cannot accept your money." It was my batman looking very happy and shaking my hand, and he would not let go until I promised to meet him next day at 'Dirty Dick's' for a drink. We had more than one that day swapping our experiences. He was married with kids. Strangely I never saw him again, although I travelled every day by bus.

H.MS King George V

Descent into Deutchland
or
"For you the war is over"

by Air Commodore Noel Hyde, CBE

"Have a good trip, Sir," said my adjutant as I gave him the key to my safe and any other of the contents of my pockets that might be of value to the enemy if I should, by chance, fall into their hands. Shortly afterwards my Manchester was heading for Northern Germany on a bright moonlit night in early April 1941. The Manchester was one of a new generation of heavy bombers. It had two large Rolls-Royce engines — the Vulture. These engines were later to be replaced by four smaller ones and the aircraft renamed the Lancaster.

My crew were borrowed. Squadron Commanders were not supposed to fly as much as did the normal aircrew and, consequently, were not allowed a crew of their own. They had either to form a scratch crew or to use that of someone else. Scratch crews were not a good thing as they were not used to working together. I shall always remember the sad case of a friend of mine, who also commanded a Manchester squadron. He formed a scratch crew with his Station Commander as Second Pilot and his Squadron Navigation, Signals, and Gunnery Leaders in other crew positions. They went off to Berlin, but did not return. Station and Squadron organization consequently suffered considerably.

On this occasion, our target was the submarine yards at Kiel. As we approached at around 20,000 feet we could see that the AA defences were quite busy. At that stage in the war, it was the practice on bomber raids to allow an interval of two minutes between aircraft over the target in order to avoid collisions. However, this provided the defences with an ideal opportunity to concentrate their efforts on one aircraft at a time. They used to co-ordinate their searchlights and 'cone' the attacking bomber, thus providing an excellent target for the AA guns. Later in the war, the boffins calculated that the risk of the single bomber being shot down was considerably higher than the probability of collision with a number of aircraft over the target at the same time. The concentration confused and divided the defences.

When we reached the target we were duly 'coned' and received the undivided attention of the heavy AA guns. While we certainly felt the frequent jolts and shudders caused by nearby shell burst, the aircraft did not appear to have suffered any serious damage until, shortly after leaving the target area, our starboard engine was seen to be on fire. Efforts to put out the fire were unsuccessful. So, in view of the probable explosion of the adjacent fuel tank, the crew were ordered to abandon aircraft, which they did, shortly to be followed by their Squadron Commander.

I discovered two things during my descent on to North Germany. One was always advised to have a tight fitting parachute harness, but a fairly loose harness was easier to use and more comfortable under normal conditions. Mine was loose, which caused considerable discomfort around the crutch during the descent. The other was the rather deceptive speed of descent. After some minutes of quiet, leisurely fall the ground suddenly rushed up at one at an entirely unexpected speed, causing a prize bruise on whichever portion of one's anatomy happened first to make contact with terra firma.

After extracting myself from my parachute, rubbing my bruises and checking on a cracked tooth, I stuffed my parachute into a ditch and headed, hot-foot, away from the area towards the north where, at distance unknown, lay the Danish border. Denmark was, of course, under German occupation, but one could expect a kinder welcome and possible help from the inhabitants. After a while, feeling somewhat tired and shaken up, I decided to hide myself during the coming day and to continue my travels on the following night. Having collected a couple of mangel-wurzels for sustenence, I entered an isolated church and established myself in the belfry. However, around dawn, it occurred to me that an empty building was a likely place to be searched for evading aircrew. So, together with my mangel-wurzels, I went off to the fields and found myself a convenient patch of brambles into which I disappeared from public view until dusk. A most cold and uncomfortable residence.

During my nocturnal wanderings of the previous night, I had noticed a signpost indicating that Flensburg was only five or six miles away. I remembered that Flensburg was a small Baltic port, so decided to go there and hide myself on a Swedish ship. I reached Flensburg in good order, but had to move around in order to find the docks. The moon was full and I had had to retain some of my flying clothing because of the cold. Consequently I felt rather outstanding and it was not long before I ran into a policeman. He looked at me rather suspiciously, but did not accost me. However, within less than a minute I passed a blonde popsie with a spotty faced boy-friend. The popsie, on seeing my Sidcot suit immediately started shouting "Terrorflieger. Terrorflieger." The policman heard this and I was promptly followed down the street by all three of them. It was not long before I was overtaken and felt the muzzle of the policeman's pistol in the small of my back, accompanied by the ominous words "Kommen sie mit!" Our little party then proceeded to the police station.

The head policeman was a large, fat man who was overjoyed at the part his police were playing in the war effort of the Fatherland. He hailed the blonde popsie as a heroine of the Third Reich and embraced her to, what I considered to be, a quite unnecessary extent. After some telephoning, a brace of feldwebels arrived and took me off to the Luftwaffe base near the town. On arrival, I was taken into the Officers' Mess to be checked over by the Kommandant. All was very formal. Having given my name, rank and number, it was appreciated that I was an Oberst Lieutenant (one up on the Kommandant, who was a major!) and the atmosphere changed a bit. Eventually I asked for some food, as I had eaten only a small portion of mangel-wurzel during the previous two days. Sandwiches and brandy were quickly produced.

After a while, further German officers started coming into the room, presumably to look at their kriegsgefangenan. They too sampled the brandy bottle and the atmosphere rapidly became relaxed. *Waffenbrudershaft* was the theme of the evening and I was given to understand that they were not necessarily Nazis, but were officers of the Luftwaffe who respected their fellow eagles. I had with me a small amount of loose change which I passed on as souvenirs. I was immediately presented with small pieces of German currency, which I welcomed as possible help with future escape purposes. The party was becoming decidedly cheerful, so I decided to decline further brandy as I thought that this might be leading up to questions that I should not answer. I was also rather worried about the Kommandant, who was becoming quite affectionate and informed me that as I was a senior officer, I should spend the night in his quarters. In the event, all went well. The Kommandant went to sleep and I had a quiet, refreshing night.

In the morning I was visited by a security officer and removed to the guardroom. My small horde of German currency was confiscated and I was despatched under guard to Ober Ursel, near Frankfurt, which was a clearing centre for Luftwaffe prisoners. Here I discovered that my crew were accounted for and I began what was to be four very frustrating years as a guest of the Third Reich.

Having been deposited at the Dulag Luft by my captors at Flensberg, I now became a formally accredited prisoner of war. Dulag Luft was a small Luftwaffe camp situated at Ober Ursel near Frankfurt. Its purpose was to obtain as much useful intelligence as possible from newly captured aircrew, and to notify the International Red Cross of their capture and condition.

On arrival, the newcomer was taken to the HQ Block and installed in a small room with a barred window glazed with opaque glass to prevent the occupant from seeing outside. Furnished with a bed, chair and small table, no reading matter and no pictures. The object being to get the inmate into a suitable mental state for interrogation. After what had probably been a rather harrowing experience, he found himself completely isolated with nothing to do except to recall his past and to wonder about his future. No reading, no writing, no talking. Nothing. Food was brought in at appropriate periods by a taciturn guard.

After a day or two of this negative existence, an interpreter in civilian clothes and wearing a Red Cross armband, would appear with a lengthy list of questions printed on a form headed by the Red Cross insignia and a Swiss address. The questions asked were of course, about subjects quite apart from the 'Name, rank and number,' which was the total information required from a POW under an international agreement. If the prisoner refused to answer these questions, which were mainly concerned with RAF organization, aircraft types and performances, he was told that this information was required by the International Red Cross and failure to provide it would almost certainly cause delay in informing the British Red Cross of his capture. He would then be left with the incomplete form in order to reconsider his decision.

Needless to say, the interpreter was not a member of the Red Cross. He was a Sonderfuhrer (Special Leader) whose job was to collect Intelligence. The Sonderfuhrer was followed, after a further period of solitude, by a superficially friendly German Luftwaffe officer, brimming over with *bonhomie* and *waffenbrudershaft*. "Just dropped in, my dear chap, to see how you are and to find out if there is anything that I can do for you. Have a cigarette. Please keep the package." The conversation would then proceed on more personal lines, such as, "Let me see, you were in --- Squadron, were you not? How is old George Brown, your squadron commander and Joe Smith — didn't he get married the other day?" The squadron number could probably be obtained from the code letters of the crashed aircraft or other items, whereas the personal details of other members of the squadron were probably obtained from letters, written or received, by other members of the squadron captured previously. The conversation would then move on to operational or technical matters, with the occasional bit of known or suspected information thrown in, such as, "How is the Wellington's undercarriage behaving now that the recent modification has been carried out?" An inexperienced and susceptible crew member could easily say to himself, "They seem to know it all anyway, so I might as well continue talking."

Eventually, in anything from a couple of days to a couple of weeks, when German Intelligence considered that they had gleaned as much useful information as possible from the individual, he was escorted to the main compound and left with his fellow prisoners.

The compound at the Dulag was very small compared with most camps. I recollect that there was accommodation for about fifty officers in wooden blocks and a similar compound for other ranks. The place acted as a staging post where newly captured prisoners became acclimatized to their new life-style, could write their first letters and get kitted out with essential clothing. The latter was almost entirely British and French uniforms captured by the Germans during the blitz. There was a large supply of French army greatcoats of a delicate light-blue colour. These were a common sight in British POW camps. Newly arrived POWs usually stayed at Dulag until a sufficient number had been collected to warrant the organization of a transfer to a main camp.

About a dozen POWs were kept permanently at Dulag. They initiated the new arrivals into their new way of life and helped them in a number of ways. Several ORs were also kept who helped with cooking, cleaning and other chores. Food was prepared centrally and the best use made of German garrison rations helped out by Red Cross parcels when available. Wines and spirits were sometimes available for purchase with *Lagergelt* (camp money). While at Dulag I had news of the birth of my younger daughter and was able to buy a bottle of ersatz rum with which to celebrate.

Lagergelt was specially designed and printed paper notes, in German currency, for use in prison camps. Under an international convention all officer prisoners had a proportion of their pay deducted at source and credited to them by their captors, who would not allow them to possess normal currency as it could be used for bribery or escaping purposes.

The Senior British Officer was Wing Commander Harry Day, an officer well known in the pre-war RAF, who had been shot down early in the war while commanding a Blenheim squadron. He was to finish the war in a concentration camp and was awarded the DSO and made an OBE for his activities. Major Johnny Dodge was another permanent resident. A most likable and unusual character. He was born an American of a wealthy family, but, having some influence with Winston Churchill, he came over to England during the 1914-18 war and was given a commission in the Naval Division, then serving in the Dardenelles. He subsequently transferred to the Army and finished the war as a well decorated Lt.-Colonel. After the war he took out naturalization papers and became involved with the City of London. With the approach of the Second World War, he joined a territorial regiment and was captured at St. Valery in France during the blitz. While being moved in a barge, full of fellow captives, he dived into the river Rhine and swam to the shore. However, he was soon recaptured by a Flak Battery. As the AA was run by the Luftwaffe, he was sent to the Dulag where he remained. In fact he *remained* under the wing of the Luftwaffe for the *rest* of the war in other camps. However, more of Johnny Dodge later on.

Another outstanding character was the son of a famous actress, a regular naval officer who had been serving in the Fleet Air Arm. He was religiously inclined and, in spite of his occupation, had become a pacifist. He used to conduct a short service on Sunday mornings and thought it proper to omit the usual prayer asking for blessings on the armed forces. This led to a slight schism, with the chaps going around saying, "We want our blessing, but John will not let us have it!"

Escape! This possibility qickly comes to the mind of the newly captured POW. His best chance would probably have been on arrival on enemy territory before capture, but few aircrew were prepared for this, as few seriously contemplated the possibility of capture. The alternatives were operational survival or the 'Chop'. In addition, of course, most arrived after a fairly traumatic experience and had no plans for evading capture. It was, however, somewhat different for those whose arrived in occupied friendly territory, where they could often receive help from the inhabitants. In Western Europe 46 RAF officers escaped after capture, while 401 evaded capture — mostly from France, where the French Resistance, at considerable risk to themselves, organized escape routes through Spain.

Efforts to escape did not appear to be a major preoccupation at Dulag, but I soon discovered that a tunnel was being excavated from underneath one of the living blocks. I managed to get myself on to the working party, but there was no urgency to get the tunnel completed, as many of the originators thought that it should not be used until the autumn when garden and farm produce would provide sustenance for the escapees. To others of us this seemed to be stretching things too far, as it was then only late spring. We made our point and it was agreed that we should break out during a moonless period as soon as possible.

Digging tunnels was an unpleasant occupation. The tunnel itself had to be kept as small as possible because the excavated soil had to be moved and disposed of. The limited air available quickly became stale as the oxygen was used up. Light was usually provided by a small lamp made of rendered fat which tended to go out as the oxygen went. Subsidence of the roof was always a major hazard and on most of the larger, more ambitous tunnels in other camps the roof had to be shored up. On this particular tunnel, I had a section of the roof fall in on me, but fortunately it was only a small amount and there was a fellow 'Kreigie' behind me who helped to pull me from under the fall.

I was rather worried that I would be shipped off to a main camp before the tunnel was completed and thus miss the chance to escape. I discussed this with Harry Day who, very decently aproached the Kommandant asking that I might stay at Dulag. This was agreed subject to an interview. I was duly taken to the Kommandant's quarters. He was a regular officer, a gentleman and a decent chap (we exchanged Xmas cards until a few years ago). I was given a drink and asked a few leading questions about aircraft development in the UK, but he did not get peeved when he did not get the answers that he hoped for. Eventually I was told that I could stay at Dulag and was sent back to the compound without an escort. My immediate reaction was to make a dash for it, but I was not prepared with maps, food, etc., and I was fairly certain that someone was watching me. So I meekly returned to my barbed wire cage.

Eventually the tunnel was completed, except for the final breaking of the surface outside the perimeter wire, and a date was fixed for the escape on the next moonless night. Johnny Dodge and I decided to go together and planned to walk south crossing into Switzerland at the Schaffhausen bulge. Most of the frontier between Germany and Switzerland in the south is formed by the river Rhine, except for a largish peice of territory at Schaffhausen which provided a land boundary that promised to be an easier crossing point than the river.

At last, the great day, or night, arrived and lots were drawn as to order of departure. The earlier the better, there was always the danger of discovery as the exodus continued and an early departure ensured a longer period of darkness in which to get well away from Dulag. Johnny and I were unlucky in being towards the end of the party. However, our turn came, so we entered the dark, narrow tunnel and edged ourselves forward, but near disaster was to come. Johnny, who was a large chap and was encumbered with food and other escaping necessities, got stuck in the tunnel. Quite apart from causing delay to those behind us, there was a definite risk of the tunnel collapsing due to Johnny's struggles to extricate himself. Anyway, the worst was avoided and a rather exhausted Johnny managed to free himself. We emerged into a calm Westphalian night shortly before dawn. We were not to see Dulag again.

We had a small escaping compass. A minute thing that had been sewn into the belt of my tunic, but we had planned to use the north - south autobahn and the railways as our main guide-lines. Pedestrians were not allowed on the autobahns, but as we were so late getting out of the tunnel, we decided to risk it for the first few miles from Ober Ursel. It was near daylight and it was important that we got as far away as possible. There was no traffic on the autobahn and no one appeared to be about on this early summer's morning.

It was soon broad daylight and as we were plodding along at the side of the road, I suddenly observed a 'Flak' battery set up on the opposite side, with a rather bored-looking sentry who was observing us in a somewhat disinterested manner. I turned to Johnny and said, "Don't look now, but someone is watching us." He glanced over his shoulder and his infantry training reacted immediately. He flung up his right arm and fell flat on his face. I helped him up and we proceeded on our way, leaving a rather surprised looking, but otherwise inactive, sentry behind us. This episode reminded us that we were taking an unwarranted risk by continuing to travel by daylight, so we left the autobahn and found an isolated bramble patch into which we went and remained for the rest of a long summer's day. We had food, but no water and consequently suffered from an acute thirst as well as boredom.

As soon as it was dark we set off heading south once more. All was quiet and peaceful until we came to a bridge, when we were brought up short by a shout *"Halt! Ich haber ein pistol in mein handt."* Even to the non-German speaker that sentence did not need translating. We should, of course, have realized that the escaped prisoner alarm would have gone out and that a bridge over the autobahn was an ideal check point. Anyway, we allowed ourselves to be recaptured by the guard on the bridge. For this, in retrospect, we found it difficult to forgive ourselves. Under those conditions it would have been unlikely for a man with a pistol to have hit us if we had made a dash for it. However, we were then escorted to the nearby Rhine Mainz airfield and, once more, to the custody of the Luftwaffe. At least, we were given several pints of ersatz coffee with which to assuage our thirst.

By the second day after the escape, the Dulag had received a number of reports from police and service units of recaptured prisoners. They, therefore, sent a bus round the countryside picking up weary and dejected kreigsgefangeners. After a homily from the German escorting officer on how disappointed the Kommandant was that, in spite of our good treatment, we tried to escape, we were deposited at Frankfurt gaol for several days. While in the gaol, we were visited individually by members of the Gestapo, who wished to discover details of our escape such as escape routes planned, equipment and whether we had had any help from German personnel. The gaol itself was really rather unpleasant. Dirty and very smelly, a rusty metal bucket for a urinal and nothing to read or to distract one. Plenty of time in which to realize one's mistakes and to curse oneself for one's failure. We soon learnt that all of our escapees had been rounded up.

After a few days we were taken by train to, what was then, the main Luftwaffe camp, Barth on the Baltic coast. This comparatively small camp, officially known as Stalag Luft I, held approximately 200 prisoners, the majority of the RAF aircrew captured at that time. A few RAF chaps had been sent previously to a camp, run by the German army, at Spangenburg. This was an old castle which had also been used to house prisoners during the Napoleonic Wars. One small story about this camp has always amused me. there was no recreational area in the schloss, so the inmates were occasionally marched down to a nearby village for a game of soccer. Usually they sang during the march, but the Kommandant decided that this should not be allowed as it suggested a high morale amongs the prisoners to the local people. The Senior British Officer put in a plea that they should, at least, be allowed to sing the British National Sports Song. The Kommandant agreed to this, with the result that the sports party could be seen and heard lustily singing "Beatox! What a delightful smell. Beatox! That every grocer has to sell," etc, etc. The German guards would nod and smile to each other, saying *"Ja. Ja. Das ist der Britischer Sport Song."*

Anyway, at this stage — summer 1941 — I was firmly established at Barth, but was not to stay there for very long.

*   *   *

Stalag Luft 1 — Barth

Barth was a comparatively small camp holding perhaps 300 POWs and situated on the Baltic coast near Rostock. At this time, summer 1941, it was the only Luftwaffe camp apart from Dulag Luft. On arrival I was welcomed with 14 days solitary confinement in the 'cooler' (punishment cell) to atone for my part in the Dulag escape.

The cooler was in the vorlager and was part of a wooden block which contained the guardroom and sick quarters. Its window was, as to be expected, covered by iron bars. However, an earlier occupant had observed that these bars were held in place by several nuts and bolts, but the nuts were on the inside of the cell. Somehow he managed to loosen them, remove the bars and get out of the window. He still had to get past a partrolling guard and out of the wired outer fence. He found that there was a small gap below the main gate and that there was a point where this had been enlarged by a rut caused by heavy traffic. When the guard's attention was directed elsewhere, he managed to squeeze himself under the gate and away. As far as I remember, he then made his way to Sassnitz from where a ferry service to the Swedish mainland operated. He made it.

In the main compound the Germans dug a deep ditch along the inside of the perimeter wire in order to prevent tunnels being dug from the compound to outside the wire. The bottom of the trench was out of sight of the Goon Boxes (watch towers at the corners of the compound, equipped with searchlights and machine-guns). It occurred to me that it should be possible to burrow the few yards necessary from the trench to the outer world at night and to put the soil behind one as one dug oneself forward. A major snag would be ventilation. One would have to make a large number of air holes to the surface and the tunnel would have to be deep enough to prevent a German sentry from decending through the roof when passing overhead on his routine patrol outside the wire. Anyway, I thought it a feasible proposition and began to plan accordingly.

Normally, an escape led to widespread searches inside and outside the camp. Outside, it was a case of alerting the police, service units, railway stations, etc. of the escape, while inside a thorough check was made of numbers and individuals, in order to establish how many and who was missing. After the count all the occupants of a compound were normally moved out to another area while a search was made of the barrack blocks for any of the missing personnel and for work or equipment that might be connected with escaping or other prohibited activities.

If my tunnelling plan worked, it would obviously be a great help if my absence was not immediately noticed. There was a small party who were planning to escape through the perimeter wire, so I decided to go into hiding if and when they got out. Our wooden barracks were erected on brick foundations and the occupants of one of the rooms had constructed a hiding place for illicit belongings under the floor of their room where a space of approximately 6×3×2 feet was surrounded by short brick walls. Just room for a normal sized chap to lie on his back. By this time we had become quite good at concealing trap doors in the wooden floors. The floor boards were cut irregularly, so that the edges of the trap door were not obvious and dust was carefully swept into the cracks when the trap was shut.

The German security staff normally included several men whose job was continually to search the prisoners' compound to find hiding places, tunnels or other preparations to escape, and forbidden articles. These were called 'Ferrets' and were to be seen poking around the camp at all hours of the day.

They were the main danger to my planned attempt to disappear.

Eventually, the perimeter wire party to break out, so into my coffin I went, and out of the compound were shepherded the remained POWs. I expected to wait for several hours, but time seemed unending and, as to be expected, the time came when I just had to relieve myself. Not easy when one has to lie on one's back, with little room to move. Previously a fellow inmate had presented me with a most unusual object to discover in a POW camp — the idea was that I could use this as a receptacle and then tie a knot at the end of it. This worked perfectly until, after more time had elapsed, the call of nature became urgent once more. The device was not fully inflated, so I thought that it would, once again, offer me relief. However, being made of rather thin rubber, my efforts to undo the invisible knot were defeated and the whole issue burst open depositing its contents all over me — shortly to be followed by the second instalment. Most unpleasant!

Shortly afterwards I heard noises outside my brick wall. These suggested that a ferret was busy searching the underneath of the block. I felt quite confident that he would not find me, until I heard scraping and tapping noises on my brick walls. These went on for some time and it became evident that he was trying to dislodge one of the bricks. Inevitably, he suceeded and an arm was pushed through the gap and began fumbling around until a dirty, gritty hand arrived on my face accompanied by an alarmed exclamation by the ferret. I managed to get out by the trap door before the ferret could get round, but, alas, there was nowhere else to hide and back I went to the cooler.

All this was too frustrating. I eventually hit on the idea of getting through the wooden ceiling of the cell and then crawling along the rafters until I was over the sick quarters. Then, with any luck, I might get down and out into the vorlager. From there I would take any chance that might offer itself, such as hiding in a vehicle that might later be going out of the camp. Alas, this was not to be. Before I had completed my trap door into the roof, I was marched out of my little cell and transported to a new army camp at Lubeck. I did hear later that an unfortunate Squadron Leader was subsequently put in this cell and, while there, my preliminary efforts on the ceiling were discovered. Poor chap, he was blamed for it and had to do an extra ten days in solitary.

Lubeck

Lubeck was a new camp as far as British POWs were concerned. Situated near the old Hanseatic port about 50 miles west of Barth, I believe that it had housed French POWs who had been repatriated, but at this time it contained British officers who had been captured in Crete and was administered by the German army. Troops captured in Crete were not very popular with the Germans as they were accused of mutilating dead and wounded German troops. The New Zealand Maoris in particular were suspect.

I believe that subsequent investigations suggested that the culprits were the native Cretans. The RAF were also unpopular for a different reason.

Shortly before my arrival, a lone Wellington bomber, that had either lost its main target or who had a few spare bombs to dispose of, apparently mistook the perimeter lights of the camp for a railway marshalling yard and promptly bombed them. By good fortune it missed the main camp, but scored a bull's-eye on the German Officers' Mess. Most unpopular.

On arrival I found myself back in the cooler in order to finish my sentence from Barth. Tapping on the cell wall led to verbal communication with the occupant of the next door cell through the cell windows. This led to the discovery that the tenant of a further cell was an old aquaintance of pre-war Cairo. A Sapper Colonel who had married one of my wife's bridesmaids. Also in the cooler block were the Kommandant's rabbits kept, presumably, to supplement his meat ration. These were looked after by the cooler guard and were fed on stale ration bread. Occasionally, a friendly guard would give us a few chunks of the bread, which, while somewhat mouldy, was edible and very welcome. Red Cross parcels had not reached Lubeck and we were on somewhat thin rations.

The Kommandant also had a large, fat tabby cat that used to go under the wire, into the POW compound. Eventually, some unprincipled, but hungry, inmates got hold of the poor pussy who was never seen again. I was told that he tasted something like rabbit, but rather stringy.

There is little more to relate about Lubeck, as soon after my release from the cooler, the whole camp was moved to Oflag VIB at Warburg near Kassel in Western Germany, where I was to have a rather longer sojourn.

After my comparatively short periods at Ober Ursel, Barth and Lubeck, I found myself in a large, well-organized Army camp that had been set up to house most of the Army officer POWs captured up to late 1941, estimated at 2,500, plus 450 orderlies. Here we had several interesting escaping attempts, on one of which, three Army officers managed to get back to the UK via Holland. During this period the Luftwaffe could not accommodate the steady stream of new POWs coming in from the rapidly increasing attacks by Bomber Command. A big, new camp was being built at Sagan in Silesia, while in the meantime, batches of RAF POWs were placed in Army camps, including Warburg where we had about 3-400.

I spent a year at Warburg before moving on once again. There followed a spell at Stalag XXB at Schubin in Poland, then off to the main Luftwaffe camp Stalag Luft III at Sagan, followed by the Marlag (Naval camp) near Hamburg and, finally back to Lubeck where we were to be released in due course by the advancing British Army.

At last the war was over for me.

The Day I Became a POW

by Gunner C. T. Randall 919419

How could one think of war in July 1939 at Bembridge on holiday with just the beach hut and rowing boat, and simple pleasures of long walks along the cliffs to Sandown, to meet other families connected with one's school and St. John's Church Southend, Catford?

Territorial Camp at Beaulieu did nothing to give thought of the conflict which was to follow within a week or so — why should it? — old worn out equipment from the First World War, old greengrocers' vans to tow the guns, and very few dressed alike, with some in civilian clothes.

Through the post I received Army form E.518 'Reserve and Auxiliary Forces Act 1939 Territorial Army — Calling out Notice'.

Gunner Randall C. T. 919419 in pursuance, etc. etc. will report to 91st Field Regiment, Ennersdale Road, S.E.13 on 1st September 1939. This was surely just a precaution — war would never come — it must be a false alarm.

And so that evening by coach to Kempton Park Racecourse. How well I recall that first night. One blanket — did one sleep on it or under it? The marble floor in the tote was so hard. Sleep was nigh on impossible. Singing 'South of the Border down Mexico Way' and 'Roll out the Barrel' seemed to carry on all night.

My unit was to be prepared to go overseas immediately war was declared — how could it? It was medium field artillery 25-pounders but alas, we had no guns. Towards the end of September some 1914/18 guns arrived. (No. 2 Gun in my troop had 'Loos 1915' on the breech.)

We set sail for Cherbourg and travelled down the peninsula to Laval where we were billeted in old barns. Our destination was of course the Belgian border, but we had no gun towers! It was thought bad propaganda to cross France with the 'Sunlight' laundry vans which had been commandeered and camouflaged. After a week or so of learning to change step on the march, followed by numerous inspections of kits which did not exist, we crossed the north of France to a small village a few miles from Lille.

For several months, time was spent on the usual army monotonous 'bull', occasionally broken by digging latrines and gun pits. The three/four day manoeuvres were great fun and most enjoyable.

Suddenly the unit was withdrawn from the line to hasten to Norway. Still

101

in France this was halted due to the complete fiasco and final collapse of that operation. The regiment remained in the Beauvais area in small villages surrounded by glorious forests. I well remember a cross-country run in which I came twentieth out of fifteen hundred men when we challenged the Royal Corps of Signals.

'The Trumpet sounded!' On my twenty-fifth birthday in May 1940 we raced to Belgium. How well I remember cutting my birthday cake with my bayonet as we crossed the border to dig in behind Brussels between Halle and Ath. I was in 'B' Troop and our guns were near a tiny village of Bellingham — I once lived in Bellingham Road, Catford.

Here as far as I was concerned only two things happened. Firstly, I experienced being under a prolonged and heavy artillery barrage and shrapnel. Secondly, I was responsible for laying a cable from 'B' Troop gun position to the observation post (OP) some four miles long running at a slight angle to the River Schelde. On returning to the gun position the line went 'diss' and I was ordered to find the break and repair. Alas, although radio silence was to have been observed it was broken by the OP who collected two signallers on the line and the signal truck picked up the other two signallers nearer the guns, leaving Gunner Randall to walk right into the advancing Germans. My heart nearly missed a beat when I climbed the water tower to find all had vanished.

Then followed a long worrying exciting never-to-be-forgotten four weeks. Making my way back I had the fortune to meet a Company of Royal Engineers from Reading and kept with them for two weeks. This unit was engaged in 'delaying tactics' — blowing bridges, etc. We were working by day and moving by night with food becoming scarce. Three times through misunderstanding with the Infantry we found ourselves on the wrong side of the bridge which had been blown. Not so clever in the dark!

Continually in close proximity to the advancing Germans in very nerve-racking. Often as we left one village, they entered. On one occasion I was asleep at the back of an estaminet when some Germans entered — believe me I have never moved so fast in my life.

So Dunkirk fell — I found myself in a small town of Cassel some twenty miles south of Dunkirk. This town was perched on a hill from which for three days we watched the German tanks pass in perfect formation — hundreds and hundreds of them. The town of Cassel was bombed, shelled and mortared — snipers had already infiltrated, and with fifth-columnists it was all hell let loose. My hide-out was a champagne warehouse. How many folk have drunk nothing but champagne for three days? Not many I bet.

On this hill there must have amassed some 1,500 men of different units. No one seemed to know what had happened. Pamphlets had been dropped giving a map of the area showing there was no escape and telling us to surrender — 'For you the War is over'.

Two officers made a brilliant on the spot plan to evacuate the town at 10 p.m. Parade was in the small cobbled square. The church clock with flames licking around its tower, struck ten, as possibly the last order to any organized fighting was given which was 'The British Army will march'. Hopes were very high and all went well for two or three days. Then every trouble began — the column were endeavouring to make the Cherbourg peninsula going south-west. Gradually the Germans set upon the 'New Contemptibles' with mopping up operation. To miss fire from a farmhouse I crawled along a ditch only to find myself facing a couple of Germans with a machine-gun. Fortune again came to my aid and a small recce carrier stopped near on to which I made a dive. This got me out of a spot of bother, but I found on going through villages I was a sitting duck for rifle fire. How I survived I do not know.

After a couple more days I made for a small forest where I found exactly 49 other men all tired and hungry. That night after the Germans had mortared us a party came through with hand-grenades. We made one bayonet charge and left at three yard intervals at 11 p.m. Again all went well for two more nights (travelling by day was out of the question, Jerry was everywhere). We found it was getting more and more difficult to probe forward, meeting small parties of Germans at every point. Having passed some Germans close by in the dark and then finding cross fire on both sides, I thought it safer to go it alone.

I was number three in this expedition and let the remaining forty-six pass me in the dark. I felt that I had had so many close shaves that it was like crossing Trafalgar Square blindfolded. One could do it once, perhaps twice or thrice, but ultimately one must get killed. The party not being able to go back, with cross fire right and left, there was only one direction. I remained in a small furrow in the ground. The remainder ran on to a machine-gun post. As dawn came the Germans advanced from several directions, and I was captured. I was searched and marched off past those that were machine-gunned. I recall asking to take one of the dead men's blanket and water-bottle. (The blanket is still in the back of my car. The water-bottle I lost in an explosion in a coal-mine in Silesia.)

After a few miles walking due east I was handed over and joined a handful of POWs. We were escorted some further ten miles, our numbers growing as we proceeded.

June and July 1940 were particularly hot. The marches of approximately twenty miles per day lasted over two weeks. The pace got slower and slower as fatigue took over. The dust was intolerable with German transport racing into France. The column extended right into the skyline. The French were to the front without guards and always appeared to have bread and bottles of wine. The buckets of water placed for us as we passed through the small towns and villages were always kicked over by the French POWs. (I still have the same opinion of the French as my father, who was in the First World War.)

We bypassed Rouen, Amiens, on to Arras, sleeping at night in hastily prepared open spaces with barbed wire. With a fortnight's marching with little food and scarcity of water, boots worn through, uniforms in many cases in tatters, life was at a low ebb. One of our night's stop was in Doullens prison. How well I remember passing Cambrai where tanks had been used for the first time in the First World War.

So at last Trier on the Rhine was reached. There we entrained in cattle trucks, over one hundred per truck. Insufficient room to sit. One man next to me died presumably of exhaustion. We were not allowed out of the trucks for three days — the stench was appalling. The heat by day was terrific. It was difficult to estimate the distance that we covered. All we knew from the sun was that it was due east. We shunted in and out of sidings continually.

Finally at midnight we were let out at Schubin, a small town in Poland. I have always felt so sorry for one fellow who died after jumping from the truck — having got so far.

The camp was some seven or eight acres, built to hold ten thousand (my number was 5655). No sanitation — just an open trench with a pole which often broke. By this time dysentry was rife. Food was one ladle of watery soup and three Polish army biscuits measuring 8" × 4" (I broke a tooth the first day).

Many of us found it difficult to stand; we were so weak and lice abounded. Thanks to the army's inoculations the dreaded typhus which wrecked Napoleon's army never swept through the camp. The camp was a perfect cess pool for any disease. Two water taps for ten thousand men. One queued night and day for water — just sufficient to avoid dehydration but not enough for washing.

Few had shaving kit — I grew a beard some seven or eight inches long and with a mass of curly hair looked just like a monkey.

A request was made of us to be registered under Geneva Conventions. The Camp Commandant informed us that it was a waste of time — the war would be over in a few days and in any case we would never see our homeland — why not let your people think you died in battle? The newspapers which the guards showed us stated that all males in England between 16 and 60 would be transported from England to work in forced labour camps. One paper stated that Hitler was having his first meal at Oxford! (not Buckingham Palace). I don't know why but I think I am right in saying that Oxford was never bombed.

After some two months we were weighed — my weight a little under five stone from nine stone — kitted out in old Polish cavalry uniforms and wooden clogs, and my party of one hundred left for Roggenfelt (Rye Field). The camp was an old village school, the village being some forty miles from Posnan. The work was demolishing the old Polish farms, constructing new German state farms and road making. The local contractor was responsible for our feeding. I still very clearly remember the first bowl of vegetable soup — thick with potatoes and carrots. Many many amusing incidents occurred at this camp — too many to relate. The first evening the interpreter escaped!

Gradually the hard, hard Polish winter set in and the next camp was Thurin, non working — almost impossible to work out of doors. All that happened at that camp of interest was being asked for volunteers to unload some trucks at the local railway shunting yard. No volunteers forthcoming, we stood for four hours in minus 30 degrees temperature — not too well clad — for the longest four hours of my life.

Suddenly, just before Christmas 1940, we moved to one of the twelve fortresses surrounding the town of Posan. From this moment it is true to say that conditions improved almost every day. First letters arrived, Red Cross parcels, and concerts of very high standard were organized. The camp had a radio, and news was received each day. It was only ten years ago that I learned from Alan Trapnell (who was then a Barrister, now a High Court Judge) in Beckenham High Street, that in fact there were three radios — one hidden in the false bottom of the swill bin. I spent days and days looking for it. The secret was well kept.

There were two thousand men in this camp. Working parties averaged thirty men. One was able to swap parties. Being a non-smoker I was able to get on lighter work for the price of a few cigarettes.

The work varied — unloading or loading scrap metal, bricks, cement, digging sand and gravel, foundation for barracks, etc. Very little room for any form of sabotage. However volunteers were requested for a 'special' job. I volunteered as it could not be worse than that work I was on. It turned out that the local farmer wanted to make four enormous potato clamps. A marvellous job — we made it last weeks and weeks — each evening returning to the camp loaded with spuds. The clamp was sabotaged 'something rotten' — little or no straw in places, the vent holes were filled with earth. When the job could no longer be kept going, the farmer reported to the Camp Commandant how pleased he was with the manner in which the men worked. The Commandant informed us that the potato clamps were the camp's allocation of potatoes for the next year! So much for sabotage!

The next camp was in the great fortress or citadel of Posnan. Posnan was a beautiful city with the Vistula or the Varta — I can never remember which — with its lovely curves winding its way through the city. The big fortress built into the rising ground just off centre to the city, had roughly ten miles of dried moat, walls forty feet high and width averaging sixty feet, with blockhouses every two or three hundred yards. Earth covered all the fortifications. It was built just after the Napoleonic wars of 1815. All the minor forts being two miles out being radial to the main fortress. A very wonderful construction. The main fort could hold half a million men. In fact the German SS held out for three months after the Russians passed it some four years later. The Russians lost forty thousand dead in taking it. Most of the Germans remain buried underneath, since the Russians covered the whole area with sand, planted trees and made a national park. (Poland was once under the sea, and the centre has several feet of sand.)

A party of two hundred was sent to the main fortress to be kept underground in retaliation for some trivial complaint purported to have been made by German POWs in Canada.

This camp, when entered down a stone staircase off a small tunnel, was like entering the Bastille — dirty, dank, dark and 'orrid. However with the aid of cigarettes purchasing cleaning material, electric light lamps, it ultimately turned out to be a good camp — cool in summer, warm in winter — I was sorry to leave it.

Space does not allow the amusing incidents that occurred — far far more amusing than many seen on television. One incident is enough. I was first to enter the underground blockhouse and spotted that the great door the size of 'Traitors Gate' at the Tower, had still got the key in the lock. This naturally I took. With easy access to the moat the walls were easily scaled with rope made from the string from Red Cross parcels. After some weeks the Camp Commandant made an unexpected tour of the quarters. To his astonishment only a handful were to be found. All the rest were in a small village a mile or so out of Posnan! He nearly had an apoplectic fit. It was difficult to convince him that most had been out every night and would soon return. He didn't take it kindly even when we told him he was such an excellent Commandant that no one would dream of trying to escape! (Amusing when one thinks of the guards doing guard duty 'two on and four off' for several weeks in the tunnel.)

Thence to Khundorf on the outskirts of Posnan — a camp of two thousand in wooden hutments. Marvellous camp. Wonderful concerts, plays, light opera — Gilbert & Sullivan. From the camp funds a grand piano was purchased for 30,000 cigarettes. The orchestra had thirty instruments, not forgetting a first class band. One of my jobs when the piano was purchased, was to arrange its transport via a factory in which I was working. Everything went wrong but finally it was accomplished. I was on the escape committee — sounds rather good — in reality it boiled down to the entertainments committee. It was through this that I volunteered for four days solitary confinement when the pianist of the Christmas Pantomime got twenty-one days solitary. Never had such a good time in POW life! The MO supplied me with two Red Cross parcels, two extra blankets, and the committee gave me several hundred cigarettes. It was a difficult task to convince the Commandant that he need not worry about the switch, identities, etc. He was worried about his own guards reporting, in which case he would be at the Russian front in forty-eight hours. The camp always checked the guards' movements with careful timing. I informed him that in the early hours of the morning the two guards were always at the top of the camp chatting for half an hour, in which time he could personally smuggle me out. The five tins of fifty cigarettes placed on his table at the interview won the day. It was an interesting experience. I thoroughly enjoyed it — no work — peace and quiet which I had not had for four years. What does one think about? In my case I tried to remember all the English counties, then the books of the Bible, etc.

The first morning a guard arrived to give me exercises — I told him in no uncertain manner that I did not require exercise and squared him in POW's usual currency. This led to every guard on the camp demanding to take me out for exercise — my fags soon ran out!

Ignoring the terrible first six months of POW life, which was physically and mentally hell, the following three and a half years were pretty good, thanks to the Red Cross, without whom possibly, some two hundred thousand of the original BEF would either be dead or in very bad health. The Red Cross was wonderful and catered for every need.

Suddenly this was all to come to an end as far as I was concerned. A party of twenty of us was sent to Upper Silesia; the first ten days at Teschen. The camp was nearly a mile long and half a mile wide, situated in the foothills to the Carpathian Mountains. The camp was an 'amassing unit' for the larger concentration camps holding possibly 50,000, with a railway line running parallel to the camp.

Our section of 200 English was wired off separately within the main camp. We were warned not to wander around the main camp unless in parties of five or six. The camp smelt, and prisoners of numerous nationalities were dying daily by starvation. One witnessed some terrible scenes.

On the first night six guards were killed by the local partisans. A train was organized to pass the camp very slowly and to let off steam. The guards in their boxes with searchlights and machine-guns were found stabbed. My worry was that we might be killed in retaliation. How thankful I was to leave the camp for coal-mining. Also during the short stay at Teschen the local partisans had stolen a large quantity of police uniforms and we learned that it was chaos in the town during the hours of darkness.

So I became a coal-miner for six months at Gleivitz and Blackhammer in Upper Silesia. No training. Straight down the mine the first day. The shifts were eight hours work on the coal face, excluding time from the bath house to the coal face. Being three miles from the shaft it took one hour to reach. The Germans were 'winning' coal without taking the normal precautions for safety — pumps were failing — one had to walk in places in three or four feet of water carrying one's boots above the head.

I worked in two different mines, one with a six foot seam, the other twenty or so. The procedure in the deep seam in Poland is to replace every cubic yard of coal with a cubic yard of sand, sand being in plentiful supply. The sand was pumped in with water and the water drained off under dams — this was why our party came to be working at this particular mine — the dam had burst killing twenty POWs and we went as replacements.

Life was really hell. We worked on a bowl of soup per day with a fifth of a loaf of bread. Germany was being bombed so heavily that Red Cross parcels rarely arrived. The only consolation I had when in the mine was that if the local town was bombed I was safe.

My worst recollection in the other mine was having to crawl for a hundred feet or so on one's stomach between the roof and the floor which was only about two feet high — I sweated with fear every time, and never got used to the ordeal. On each side of this area the coal face resumed its normal height of six feet. Frightening to see pit props one had erected, say three days earlier, crushed to pulp as the roof descended. The roof-falls in the near distance were also frightening. I had a number of very close accidents but thankfully, as usual, my luck held. Where the coal seam was only three to four feet thick, whilst very safe, I found it agony not being able to stand for long hours while shovelling coal in a sitting position. Thank heavens for being of small stature. The shovels had handles about a foot in length. Once a German overseer came at me with a coal pick and for a minute or so I had a running battle with him. Me being small and he being enormous I had a great advantage, and fended off each blow with my small heart-shaped shovel until other POWs arrived and stopped the pitched battle. I really think the Jerry was out to kill me.

After one long shift with an extra hour off for Christmas Day, we returned to the camp. Great excitement — "Draw your soup, the camp moves in one hour."

All were well aware through the radio that the Russians were making steady advances and it was now only a matter of a few months before the war would be over. Since the Germans were getting short of coal we were required to march across Poland, Sudetenland into Germany, to work in German mines.

Two thousand of us marched out of the camp in temperatures of well below thirty degrees of frost. My pack — should it be food or clothing? I voted food. I had hidden under the floor boards some 70 tins of sardines brought from the previous camp — with chocolate and three army emergency rations consisting of nine highly vitimized squares each. I calculated I had enough food for three months if the chance of escape should ever occur.

We marched for exactly forty-eight hours in a blinding snowstorm. The ground was so hard with snow and ice that with the heavy pack it was difficult or impossible to stand upright. At the beginning George (who is fit and well and lives in Liverpool) and I kept at the front of the column, which in the 48 hours only covered fifty miles. I had, at great expense, bought two or three escape maps — made of silk. I believe they were meant for airmen and were coded for escape routes connected with the underground movement. I am not sure of my facts, but from certain close observation of certain lettering I am sure I am right.

Our guards lost their way and contacted an Artillery unit who were taking up gun positions. They asked who we were and suggested that all be shot. This was rather worrying. What if it had been SS or Gestapo? Orders would have had to have been obeyed! This incident made us determined to escape if the opportunity arose.

We deliberately moved to the rear of the column — the guards were now beginning to feel exhausted. Our moment came as this long straight road, or rather track, came close to a typical Polish forest. We were now some five miles from Rattibor on the Oder. Once over, no chance of getting back. Now or never. I made a dash in the line of an arc to the forest, having arranged to remain in the area for twenty-four hours. I reckoned that with the terrible cold, and the physical state of the guards, the chances of getting shot were small in running about two hundred yards. If the guards kept their gloves on it would be difficult, if not impossible, to fire in those climatic conditions. Gloves taken off would give me those extra seconds needed for the safety of the forest. That was my theory — it worked — only one shot fired and that some yards off! George Martin took his opportunity in a similar fashion some two miles further on with equal success, and we linked up an hour later, meeting in a woodman's hut. We both had recovered our packs which had been dropped before the 'run'. The hut and the forest seemed comparatively warm after the long march in a blizzard in open country. We had no light, but managed to open a tin and make plans.

The first difficulty encountered was that we had escaped into a military zone. The Germans had possibly several divisions in the area. Secondly we decided to discard our hidden civilian clothes as it was considered safer to bluff it out in British uniform. The normal routine of moving from farm to farm across Poland proved impossible. Our luck turned when making enquiries in a small town. A very old man suggested that we made contact with two young girls — he had observed that a number of men had been to their house and disappeared — he would say no more! It turned out that the two girls aged about nineteen were Jewesses who had seen their parents beaten to death by the Gestapo, and for five years had had to work in a labour camp. They were part of an underground movement and were responsible for aiding well over one hundred escapes of important political prisoners. Even had they known who we were, normally they would never have told us of their work, but with the advance of the Russians to the north, their line of communication was broken. They hid us in their cellar for two weeks. Alas, the SS or chiefly the Gestapo, combed the village and dragged families out to be shot. We informed the girls that it was not right for us to stay in these circumstances, for if we were found they would be shot on the spot. They were prepared to take their chance, but we insisted on moving.

On our map they showed us a safe small town some fifty miles away with a reliable address. How to get there? Movement by day was impossible, with German troops everywhere, by night the roads were guarded, with troop movement, tanks, guns, etc. Cross country appeared physically impossible. To our surprise after long arguments, one started off with us just after dark. We followed her with great difficulty as we were carrying heavy packs probably weighing sixty pounds. After approximately six of seven miles we spotted a dark figure approaching us from the corner of a pine forest. I was frightened out of my life until I heard the jabber jabber of Polish, which was too quick for me to understand. Our guide bade us goodbye leaving us with the figure who was to be a new guide. This change of guides occurred about six times. We gathered from this that this was part of the old escape route and organized by radio signals. Presumably if one of the guides was found more than a few miles from his/her home it would be difficult to give a satisfactory explanation.

After several days of trial and tribulation we continued eastwards, finally finding ourselves in the middle of a tank battle — a very frightening experience. To be between two armies with tanks tearing around spitting fire in all directions was terrifying. At last the Russians pushed through — a sigh of relief — we were safe, free, and in Allied hands. Were we Hell!!! Our troubles were about to start in earnest. What to do? Where to go? A completely new set of problems now raised their ugly heads. Conversation with the Russians seemed impossible. Luck came our way when I discovered a Russian who could speak French. I managed to get him to write down who we were and what we intended to do, key words like bread, soup, etc.

We were now in the far south-east of Poland. Three or four hundred miles to the north were Norway or Sweden; Moscow was about four hundred miles north-east, if my geography was right, south were the Carpathian Mountains in which we knew the partisan forces were operating, and in any case we considered that we were not physically fit to negotiate them. It was madness to follow the advancing Russian army — due west. What would happen when the advance was blunted say on the German border? We might be months and months. North, south, east or west?

We decided to follow the railway track which cut around the Ukraine going south-east. The line had been taken by the Germans and retaken by the Russians and was in a deplorable state. Every bridge had been blown. Whoever held the railway held the terrain for hundreds of miles. Over this line some of the bitterest battles had been fought — it was the key to the whole of the southern flank of the Russian Army.

We proceeded slowly, covering some ten miles per day until I spotted a small sledge in a bakery. We smashed down the door, and with our packs on the sledge, managed to increase our distance each day to nearer fifteen miles.

Our *modus operandi* was to endeavour to keep clean and well shaved — not easy by any means. Fortunately our uniforms were in excellent condition. Our boots almost new. Like all armies, the Russians had divisional signs in each town leading to the front lines. We used to march boldly in step into the military quarters, salute the orderly on duty and present him with that valuable piece of paper which had our particulars, which resulted in either shelter or soup and bread.

So we trudged on for three months. With the terribly low temperatures and thick hard snow one might have been in the Arctic. We experienced some interesting and horrible sights. One could see very clearly where some of the tank battles had waged. Hundreds had been gathered into 'scrap yards'. That awful stench of burnt out tanks still prevailed. Then we passed two or three hundred yards of dead bodies, the ground being so frozen that it was not possible to bury them. Nearly all were stripped of boots and clothing — the bodies were piled about eight feet high by twelve feet across. A dreadful sight, impossible to expunge from one's memory.

All went exceptionally well — we learned from experience as we progressed. The language was the greatest problem or barrier. Very few Russians had ever heard of England and pointing to a map meant nothing. We usually said we were 'Americanisch' which rang a bell as there was so much American equipment about.

Finally we arrived towards the end of March in Odessa — very, very pleased with our accomplishment in covering some seven hundred miles. Applying the same drill as before we entered a military establishment and after much waiting for some unknown reason, finally marched off between two Russian guards about two miles to the outskirts of the city. There we were placed in a gaol/prison, not very extensive. It might have once been a police prison. I shall never know. Here we were placed in a small cell with almost no lighting and certainly no heat. We both lost sense of time — it was about ten days in all. I had still 250 cigarettes left. Did one bribe the guard with fifty fags with a promise of more? Or a hundred, or go plonk with the lot? We argued for some time on this tricky point — so difficult to understand the feelings and mentality of Russians — French, Germans, Japs or Spanish; yes, but not the Russians. I felt that my luck had held for over five years. Why should it desert me now? So after a long story, our guard did not lock the cell door. Was it a trap to shoot us on the excuse that we were escaping and then take our watches (which we always kept out of sight) and boots which would have fetched a fortune? All went well again, and after scaling three small walls we were free once more. by this time we were unkempt, dirty and scruffy. We marched straight through Odessa to the docks — not a difficult task, as all the roads appeared to run straight and parallel. Although we passed several military quarters we were never challenged, even on entering the docks.

What a heavenly sight to us, almost past human understanding. A Red Ensign fluttering on a vessel which turned out to be the *Highland Princess*, of 23,000 tons.

A long story here — a party of British who were in hospital in Poland were released by the Russians some three months after we had made our escape and had travelled across the Ukraine by train. By now the line had been fully repaired and made operational.

It still worried us — the Germans had always said that Britain and America would join forces with them and turn on the Russians. It seemed to me quite logical. Had it happened I would have then been 'enemy' and would not be writing this saga. Therefore to me the most beautiful and exciting sound in my life, was to hear the rasp of the anchor being drawn up in Odessa and then we were out of the Black Sea.

So now we knew not where, or cared where, we were heading, the boat sailing under sealed orders. By watching the sun and passing through the fantastic Aegean Islands and turning south, it became clear that it was odds on Egypt, which proved to be right. The Mediterranean was clear of all enemy craft. Lying on deck, sunbathing with not a ripple on the sea — well one could have easily felt one was in Heaven.

Four fantastic days in Egypt — regrettably no money. On approaching the military authorities they had never heard of the 91st Field Regiment. Where was my pay book? What, no Army Pay Book? — never heard of such a thing! I informed some RTO officer, who annoyed me with his handkerchief tucked in his sleeve, that I had been fighting for nearly five years and Army Pay Books were well down the list of priorities. George and I proceeded to the native quarter (we later learned not a wise thing to do) where we flogged our underwear, scarves, and pullovers. With the proceeds I bought a small table-cloth as a souvenir — had a wonderful time handling money for the first time in 4½ years — (strange feeling) — walking around Simon Artz, the only reputable store in Port Said.

With the few akkers left on the last evening, we hailed a horse-drawn landau, and told the driver to take us around the town until the money ran out. In fairness to the Arab, he did us well.

And so to Naples, again another vessel, and on to Gibraltar, where we waited for a convoy to be formed. The crew were livid with the authorities. Every time they had left Gibraltar, the Spanish informed the Germans who were still in the U-boat pens on the west coast of France, in particular St. Nazaire.

What a wonderful sight to see Gibraltar 'Grand and Grey', part of our mighty Empire. One felt mighty proud as we sailed past into the Atlantic.

Still our troubles were not over. Our convoy, protected by two destroyers and a couple of corvettes, was set upon. The whole convoy was badly crippled. How frightening are depth charges. I asked a member of the crew how near the nearest depth charge was since it was in darkness and we were below decks. He said two hundred yards. To me it sounded, and felt like two yards. Very frightening — but like everything else, not so worrying if you know what is happening.

So we lay off the Welsh coast until the heavy mist rose. Thence into Britain.

Then the 'army bull' commenced — so annoying when it was carried out by those who had never left England or done any fighting. The two hundred of us got very irate, and let the authorities know in no uncertain terms.

We were promised a month's leave and double rations, and to be in units near our homes. I was sent to a unit some twenty miles north of Newcastle! George received a notice to report to a unit which was going to the Far East. It was only by the intervention of his Member of Parliament that he was taken off the boat at the last minute.

The army staff could stand us no longer, and after reports to higher authority we were given a list of some dozens of Depots, and told we could take our choice. I chose Crystal Palace — partly on sentimental grounds as my father had his training there for the Tank Corps in the first war!

Lots and lots of amusing experiences here — 'Dad's Army' had nothing on it. I volunteered for a job which necessitated the use of petrol, spraying in rotation the 50,000 motor cycles distributed around the old stands. It was a mixture of lanolin and petrol. I had a car before the war. I felt sure His Majesty would not mind Gunner Randall having just enough to run the car. I had a good many quart beer bottles hidden in the Crystal Palace grounds; later the contents found their way to my petrol tank.

After a time it was suggested as the war in Europe was over, it was time that we attended educational classes. Fair enough, but to be taught by a 'Buck Sergeant' who could hardly read or write (possibly a little exaggerated) did not appeal to me. So I suggested to four of five ATS that ice-skating at Purley was much more beneficial. I met Laura, got engaged, and after six months we married at Hayes Church. We have now two children, and three grandchildren — God bless them.

*   *   *

The idle thoughts of an idle ex-gunner.

Firstly I was the only one in my Regiment not to return after Dunkirk. I still attend the 'Beer' troop reunion each year — some thirty still attend. I am still conscious of how lucky I was to have gone through the war without a scratch.

How grateful I remain to the Red Cross who were so wonderful. Thanks to those parcels my health has never suffered one iota.

During the years behind barbed wire I learnt to play Bridge to a very high standard possible County.

I read a number of classical novels — Walter Scott and the like.

I devised a simple code to let my parents know whereabouts in Poland my camp was situated. My father had an enormous map of Poland — he found it interesting when I was moved from one camp to another, some fifteen in all — it was done by initials — Mr Gn Randall E.S. E.N. (Gnesen). This slow process with one letter each week made it quite exciting for my parents. To assist I would mention that the new camp seems much 'warmer', i.e. move southwards, etc. Surprising how much one could get past the censor.

I was able to report that the French in the early days were wearing the British uniforms sent for us by the Red Cross. The Red Cross thought this was happening, and thanked my parents for confirming. Later all the uniforms were taken from the French.

A burglary, or break-in was organized by a party from our camp who attended the main Stalag — a request had come from General Fortune, the senior officer captured with the First BEF to destroy certain records — photographs and fingerprint records, to assist with one of the officers' great escapes.

Three years ago I visited Poland with an official party of one hundred to 'celebrate' Poland being freed by the Russians thirty-five years previously.

Of this expedition I could write a book. Searches for old camp sites — standing in the square at Warsaw (about ten times the size of Trafalgar Square) between possibly 50,000 Russians and 100,000 Polish troops — the laying of the wreath at the Unknown Warrior's grave. Our simple services — a POW, the Padre, a Bugler, three British Legion members and their banners, a Scottish Piper and a Chelsea Pensioner, were among our party.

A visit to the British Embassy as guests for the evening. The Palace of Culture — Chopin's Memorial, 1,000 miles of coach ride, two journeys by plane, entertainment, a police escort put at our disposal — how helpful they were.

I visited the brother of a famous Polish heart specialist who lives in England. Seeing for oneself the conditions the Poles live in — pitiful and sad. How I admire them — a marvellous nation.

Where some of our camps had been in the country, we found dual carriageways and ten-storey blocks of flats.

To be present at Czestochowa Monastery, the home of the Black Madonna, the first Sunday after the Russians swept through to revisit it. On informing a priest who the ten of us were, he drew the screens across the Lady Chapel, and in very broken English asked us to kneel while he said a couple of short prayers of thanksgiving for our survival — how moving — many a tear dropped, as on many other serious occasions. We visited a very tiny torture and extermination camp, ten times more dreadful than Auchwitz. Our simple ceremony had to be cut short as no one could sing 'O Valiant Hearts' or speak the prayers. The bugler was hard put to sound the Last Post and Reveille. It was some hours before the usual wit and humour flowed again in the coach.

The two girls who had hidden us after our escape had moved from the town of Krakow without leaving their new address. George and I had never properly thanked them for all they did for us due to circumstances beyond our control.

One day we were entertained by the Polish Army — most impressive, enjoyable and amusing.

Another day, when arriving by plane at Posnan, we were met by some of the old underground and partisan forces — eager to find if there was anyone present whom they had assisted.

Last November, I attended a POW reunion at the Fairfield Hall, Croydon. What an evening! At the entrance there were four dressed as German guards, tin hats complete. Not a smile on their faces. (The Jerries have very little sense of humour.) Later they appeared on the stage and played their part well to loud ovation. The guest of honour that evening was the Commandant General of the British Red Cross. She was in charge of affairs in Egypt and had met the *Highland Princess* as the vessel docked. Ambulances, nurses, etc. — all seemed to be unnecessary since all seemed to have recovered from whatever they had had!

This charming lady had arranged a special concert in our honour. At the end of the performance she was carried shoulder high around and around the concert hall. I was one who helped. An evening never, never to be forgottten — remember that the 200 men had had no contact with women for over four years. She and her assistants were marvellous — seemed to us just like angels.

At the reunion I mentioned the fact that I was one of the first to arrive at Port Said. She said she well remembered being hurtled around the hall by the POWs. A most charming and gracious woman — now retired.

The tales of searches, in and out of camp. Searches for the wireless. Changing the labels on the Red Cross tins and then selling them to the Germans. Keeping the old tea leaves and adding straw from the palliasses, resealing carefully and exchanging for bread — I wonder what the guards' wives thought of 'English tea'?

Where can I stop? I could go on and on and on. . . .

"I Was at the Party, but Did Not Stay"

The Story of an Australian Sailor

by G.J. Evans

I joined the Navy in 1936 when there was a bad depression all over the world and no work available. I had various trips on many ships, finally travelling to the UK to commission the *Perth*. The ceremony was held under the Royal auspices of HRH Princess Marina who later lost her husband in a tragic air disaster in Scotland.

We travelled across the Atlantic to New York and then to the West Indies, but on the 3rd September 1939 we were at war with Germany once again. At this point I had travelled some 22,000 miles on a real Cook's tour, but from this point on it was a different ball game. Action stations seemed to be on every couple of hours with submarine scares, and every sight of smoke in the distance became an enemy warship. We soon settled down however, and the war routine became the norm, only at evenings did you feel the nearness of danger.

We did two convoys up the English Channel and returned to the West Indian base, being caught in a terrifying cyclone in the Bermuda Triangle which crushed our lifeboats to matchwood, forcing us to berth, where I was put into hospital suffering from enteric fever. After recovering from this I was shipped to Canada via the Canadian National Line *Lady Hawk*, which was torpedoed on some later trip with the loss of twelve lives. I arrived in Canada and went into the Stadacona Barracks then on to an armed merchant cruiser, RMS *Alunia*, and was ready to sail when a very powerful fleet bringing gold to America for munitions arrived, and I was transferred to the battleship *Warspite*. We were three days out on our return trip to England when we were sent north to search for the *Admiral Scheer*, and it was up through the Denmark Straits inside the Arctic Circle. We travelled across to Spitzbergen and Murmansk areas with only 1½ hours of daylight each day, but missed her as she was hiding in the fiords of Greenland; it had sighted us a couple of times. Whilst we were there the rest of the convoy was sailing back to England not without incident however, as the *Rodney* was struck and damaged by a mine.

The *Warspite* docked in Greenock and I was put ashore on to a train bound for Glasgow, London and Portsmouth for a sojourn in Haslar hospital, to recover from the traumatic effects of the fever I had contracted in the

Bermuda hospital.

I was shipped to Plymouth to join the *Colombo*, a light cruiser bound for the East Indies, and as we pulled into Gibraltar after the usual rough crossing of the Bay of Biscay, which always sorts out the men from the boys, I went ashore for a shower at the barracks. The next week I had poisoned feet from acute dermatitis, and was confined to my bunk. We cruised the Mediterranean for some weeks with the usual action stations each day, landing at Malta, Alexandria and Suez, through the Canal and down to Aden, Colombo and Singapore. More cruising around the numerous islands, now Indonesia. With the advent of tropical conditions large sores took over on my body and the flesh came off with my underclothes and so I was taken back to hospital up near the causeway until I recovered.

They asked me to obtain a passport and civilian clothes and put me on the *Gorgon*, a Blue Funnel Line ship to Australia. I arrived in Perth a week later, and then made the three day train trip to Melbourne, where I was discharged. I was called up by the Army the next week but was rejected the same day. To summarize it, I had travelled some 60,000 miles in some of the most dangerous seas in the world during a war and had never been involved in a serious action, so how do I know even now whether I am a coward or a potential hero?

I went back to civilian life, and after a variety of employments, finally became a Director of my own Company and retired through ill health in 1973, I have since suffered a heart attack, but continue stubbornly to survive. One learnt the futility of conflict, and now lives only for the pleasure of watching one's grandchildren try to survive in a potentially much more dangerous era than that faced by their forebears. We did not have to contend with nuclear warfare or the frightening pollution problems that they have today. We can only hope that they will be able to look back forty years, as I have done.

From Boy to Man, in a Short Space of Time

by John Sheppard

This is the story of a soldier from Sydenham, starting from the green of Wells Park to the different green background of the Burmese jungle.

The early training received as a boy and youth with the Scouts, helped considerably with the map reading, living rough in the open, lighting a fire without a match. The general toughening-up process of the Scout Movement hardened him so that he could live the life of a soldier and survive, in one of the most difficult campaigns of the war fought by the 14th Army. From Rover Scout Johnny Sheppard to Regimental Sergeant-Major of the 1st Battalion, Queen's Royal Regiment.

It was September 1939. The sirens sounded — I experienced the first painful civilian fear of war, and wrote on the back of a cigarette packet 'Dark war clouds over Europe — what is to be?'

Soon it was the first introduction to barrack life at Guildford. Learning the art of war, how to kill, and the sheer arrogance of the English and the British Army. They started to teach us German — *'Ve zind zoldateden in der Berzatzungen Armee'* — the next day the storeman said, "What size topee do you want, Mate?" — haven't a clue — and it's off to India!

A quick dash by night to Dover, across France to Marseilles, and then on the troopship to India. The fantastically romantic voyage through the Suez Canal — watching the bum boats that came out to meet us, with natives trying to sell their wares and make a quick buck — the flying fish leaping out of the Indian Ocean — the arrival in India, and the long train journey in a temperature of 117 degrees to the town of Allahabad.

We cut our teeth on riot control, suffered from heatstroke and dysentery, survived the soakings during the monsoons, and then off to the North-West Frontier to fight the Pathans. On to Peshawar, and the first insight of a massacre of 150 dead — men stripped of all human dignity.

On to Assam for special jungle training, and to learn the technique of survival, how to ambush and how to kill. A long boat trip across the water again to Chittagong, and then a march where you begin to understand the privations and hardship of war — what it meant to suffer from thirst and develop blisters. The marching at night over the Nagedauk Pass into Arakan,

118

Burma, to take up defensive positions in the jungle. The propaganda dished out was that the Japs were small, slit eyed, and couldn't hit a haystack. The patrols were sent out in the morning — the Japs caught them in the paddy field in the cross fire, and nine men were dead. We followed the Japs back killing one we caught — he was 6ft 3 ins from the Imperial Guard — so much for the little men with slit eyes. It was as well to know the size of your enemy — we became more cautious.

The Japs began an offensive and the 7th Indian Division was surrounded. It became survival — to kill or be killed. I looked at the range of mountains and thought could we cross them and get back? It did not happen, and we carried on fighting to Buthidaung. The dead were a common sight by now — both sides — British, Japs and Indian — all a bloody mess — men fighting an invisible enemy in the green foliage, dressed in green, with green faces — all dead men stinking and rotten turning green — distorted shapes of what were once human — all left to rot and be eaten by ants and flies. The horrors and reality of war.

The rain in the monsoons, the sweat from the heat, the mosquitoes, the malaria, the beri-beri, the dysentery — all were taking their toll of the men — they were dropping like flies — some lucky ones were flown out when reinforcements were flown in, but the tide was slowly turning. The killing rate was on our side, and the Japs were being defeated.

Some of us were sent back to Assam for a rest after 18 months in the jungle. The Nagedauk Pass had been opened again by relief forces, and we were able to march out for a rest — on to a jungle airfield to the Dakotas waiting — "If a Jap plane attacks poke your Bren-gun through the porthole window and fire the whole magazine at it!" — what a hope, we lost three plane loads of troops.

The big Japanese offensive was about to take place in India. Kohima had been taken by the Japs, except for the part of Jail Hill being valiantly held by the Royal West Kents. The 1st Queen's now seconded to the 2nd Division took up positions overlooking Kohima. We were ordered to advance, and after a sleepless night and a lot of rum, faced the enemy and hell.

The barrage by British guns and planes had been tremendous. My 3rd Platoon of D Company advanced to the base of the hill. What a waste. I watched my three Sergeants go, then my Company Commander with a bullet in his guts. Private Smith ran towards me blinded, blood gushing from his eyes. I was one of the few survivors of my Company, and tried to organize a stretcher party to take the wounded back. Despite the carnage and living hell, we were successful and Jail Hill was held taken by two new Divisions — the first real major defeat for the Japs.

The dead had to be buried. The bodies had been bombed, shelled and mutilated over and over again in the final assault — mute spectators of the victory. It was no easy task to pick up what remained of your friends and comrades, and bury them in sheltered graves. I had to remove the identification tags covered with crawling maggots. Such are the glories of war.

The words on the Kohima Memorial are: 'Tell them when you go home. For their tomorrow we gave our today'.

From that moment my brain shut off. I cannot remember going on to the Chindwin crossing with the reformed Company and Battalion — I have no memory at all of the next three months before I was repatriated via a jungle staging camp and out to Bombay and home via Liverpool.

No young man ever experienced more travel, more adventure, more pathos and sadness in a five year span — from a youth I became a man. I would not have missed the experience, but I could have done without some of it. At least, remarkably, I survived.

"We are Also at War"

The Story of an Australian Soldier

by Eric Lukeman

In 1939 the umbilical cord which tied Australia to the Mother Country was intact. The Statute of Westminster (1931) was not ratified by Australia until 1942 under Prime Minister John Curtin with retrospective effect to 3rd September 1939. Since then the Australian Government decides whether or not this country is at war. On 3 September 1939 our then PM Robert Menzies said that as England had declared war on Germany it was his 'melancholy duty' to announce that we were also at war.

This came as no surprise. Australians had for years been aghast at the rantings of Hitler and found it hard to disbelieve stories of brutalities and persecutions by his regime. Although it was hoped some sanity might prevail no one really believed a war would be avoided. Even so, preparations had been neglected in the forlorn hope, it seems, that the policy of appeasement pursued by Britain's PM Neville Chamberlain would somehow succeed. Stories appeared in some sections of our Press playing down the military strength of Germany and ridiculing any suggestion of a threat from Japan. Mussolini's Italy was dismissed in similar vein and the policy of 'wait and see' was fostered as though time was on our side.

The 'Phoney' War

Even after the declaration of war there was an air of unreality. The lull which followed the fall of Poland led us to hope the war was 'phoney' after all. It was fondly thought that the French Maginot Line was impregnable and a popular song predicted that we would soon 'Hang out our washing on the Siegfried Line'. Nobody wanted to think the German 'Line' might be impregnable!

In spite of the apathy recruitment went on in Australia, as elsewhere, and men were drawn from their normal lives and from the reservoir of the unemployed. My elder brother was casually employed at the time and, between jobs, he too joined up. It soon became apparent that there was not enough camps to receive all the recruits and a temporary makeshift was conceived; that of the 'Day Boys'. My brother slept at home and went each day by tram to a local sports ground. There were no uniforms and no weapons so they drilled in civvies and used broom handles as substitutes for rifles.

121

122

These conditions improved especially after Germany's conquest of Norway, followed by the fall of the Netherlands, Belgium and France and Italy's belated entry into the war (as Mussolini believed, on the winning side).

The Situation Becomes More Serious

On the day Italy entered the war I responded to a call for volunteers to guard strategic places. I was 17 at the time, and could have been described as 'wet behind the ears'. In the 1920s and 1930s Australia received large numbers of Italian migrants and the authorities were not sure how they would react. Another youth and myself were given pick-handles and entrusted with the protection of a small bridge over a canal. We spent a long, uneventful night and I can recall wondering whether, even under extreme provocation I could actually hit someone like the local Italian greengrocer over the head with a pick-handle. The question remained hypothetical luckily, and there was no trouble anywhere as far as I know. As our troops discovered in the Middle East the Italians had no wish to fight us. The known Fascists in Australia were rounded up and interned and the remainder of the Italian-born population carried on peacefully for the duration of the war. By this time divisions of our volunteer army, the AIF, were in the Middle East and Malaya, our small Navy was doing its bit around the world and thousands of our fittest, keenest young men were in the RAAF training in Canada.

News From Britain

Winston Churchill was heard with hope and compassion and we listened anxiously to BBC news broadcasts and eye-witness accounts of actual air combat over Britain. Australians, my mother included, sent parcels of food and clothing to Britain at this stage and for quite a long time after the war was over. I vividly remember hearing news of the bombing of Coventry and the brutal threat made by Hitler that every city and town in Britain would be 'Coventrated', a new word he cynically coined to describe the awful power of his Luftwaffe. The dreadful consequence for Germany was the destruction of their lovely city of Dresden towards the end of the war. Knowing this my wife and I were deeply moved when we visited Coventry in 1980 and saw the motto 'Father Forgive' in the ruins of the old Cathedral and heard about the Society of the Cross of Nails. The theme of reconciliation linking Coventry and Dresden today would not have been thought possible at the height of the Battle of Britain and for some time after, when the struggle for survival and victory was paramount.

Enter Japan

The Japanese attack on Pearl Harbor and their apparently invincible advance southward brought war closer to Australia than ever before in our short history. It seemed only a miracle could save us from invasion. Hope of that miracle was personified by US General Douglas MacArthur who arrived to assume command of all Allied forces in the South Pacific. He had made a solemn commitment to return to the Philippines from which he had been driven after an heroic and bloody battle. Our long-cherished belief that Britain would stand between us and any enemy from Asia was shattered when Singapore fell and two of the Royal Navy's finest ships *Repulse* and *Prince of Wales* were tragically sunk. Britain was fighting for its life in Europe and it was realistic for Australia to see the USA as our only chance of holding the Japanese. This was justified when a Japanese task force was defeated in the Battle of the Coral Sea and Australia's east coast was saved from attack and possible invasion.

I became a soldier
    In 1941, just before Japan entered the war, Australia had an election and a change of Government. Our new PM was John Curtin who immediately put the country on the path it was to follow until 1949. Rationing and control of every essential activity was brought about and we experienced a period of unity and consensus unparalleled before or since. As I had reached the age of 18 I was called up, together with most of my friends. We were needed to help fill the yawning gap left by the absence of our older brothers overseas. The 8th Division had been captured in Singapore and our other divisions were totally involved in the Middle East as part of the Allied Army fighting the Italians and Germans. Our small population and extensive coastline left us vulnerable to an enemy if it could get close enough to attack. My brief introduction to Army life was two weeks drill and no combat training. We were allotted to various units, most going to the infantry. I found myself in the artillery and part of a group of 40 boys my own age led by Captain Walklate, a World War 1 veteran. He wore a Lugar pistol taken from a German he captured in France in 1916 and this really made an impression on us. We were told we were a battery and our guns were on the high seas. They were the latest 'Twin 6-pounders'; coastal guns to be installed inside Sydney Harbour. Soon afterwards the bad news reached us that the ship had been sunk off the coast of Africa. So we were like the famous 'Pub with no beer'— a battery with no guns!

Bare Island
    In 1770 Captain James Cook described the entrance to Botany Bay where he anchored his barque *Endeavour*, as follows:

> 'To sail into it keep the south shore on board until within
> a small bare Island which lies close under the north shore. . . . . .'

In the nineteenth century when an invasion by 'the Russians' was feared, this island was made into a fort. Huge ungainly muzzle-loading cannon were installed. Lord Kitchener later condemned it because the fort was too far inside

124

the bay and as the Russians or no other 'aggressor' arrived the fort became a war veterans' home. Today it is a museum.

But in 1942 we were there — 40 young recruits led by a fatherly Captain (with his Luger) among retired veterans of the Boer War. These old campaigners told us earnestly we should go back to using horses because machines were unreliable.

We were not there to man old cannon of course. Soon two small guns arrived from naval stores. They were 3-pounders dated 1893! As weapons they were almost useless as they were worn smooth inside the barrel but they made a lot of noise. People living near by must have thought we had something very powerful indeed on the island and I suppose it was part of the army's plan to keep us occupied and make the populace feel more secure. We realized this was all we had so we made the best of it for the time being.

Port Hacking

I was posted a few miles south of Botany Bay to a battery guarding the entrance to Port Hacking. Following are extracts from a paper I read to the Sutherland Historical Society in 1971 entitled 'Fortress Shire':

Back in 1942 when it seemed almost certain the Japanese would attack Sydney, I was attached to a battery at Oak Park, Cronulla. . . .

Our 'powerful' armament was two Hotchkis quick-firing 3 pounders and a Lewis gun! . . . . The CO gave orders from a command post on top of Oak Park Pavilion.

The guns were 1896 vintage, at least more modern by three years than those on Bare Island which I had just left.

We had telescopic sights too and could expect to be more accurate than Bare battery which had open sights. Even so, any target would need to be closer than 2,000 yards for our shots to be effective. In any case, action would be confined within the narrow entrance to Port Hacking, and from the small number of shells supplied the army obviously expected a quick result . . . .

The command post, a concrete room with independent foundations, still graces Oak Park Pavilion and doesn't seem out of place even now. In fact the battery was made to appear as part of the bathing scene by rather novel camouflage. The gun emplacements had wooden doors painted brightly in candy-stripes to suggest kiosks and, from a distance they did look convincing, even if picnickers laughed.

Each evening a launch from the Naval Auxiliary Patrol emerged from Gunnamatta Bay and after a sweep of Bate Bay, anchored off Jibbon Beach for the night — more of a sitting duck than a sentinel during the hours when action was likely to occur.

Barbed wire was laid around the foreshores but the sea has since removed it . . . .

The Time of Greatest Danger

Our comrades in the infantry were fighting the Japanese hand to hand in the jungles of New Guinea on the Kokoda Trail, the path over the Owen Stanley Range. They were falling back to Port Moresby which was subjected to continuous air attack. At Milne Bay on the south-eastern tip of New Guinea some of our boys had actually defeated a Japanese landing attempt and this proved to be significant. Bombs had fallen on Darwin, Broome and Townsville, the heaviest damage being in Darwin.

Japanese submarines were sinking ships daily along the east coast and midget submarines were sunk inside Sydney Harbour itself. A large sub surfaced off Sydney and Newcastle at night and shelled the two cities, miraculously causing very little damage and no serious casualities. The war was then very close indeed to home — it was no longer something happening afar. Indeed this marked the highest point of the Japanese attack and from then on the tide of war was in our favour.

We were given the chance to transfer to the AIF which meant volunteering for service anywhere in the world and almost all of us volunteered.

I was transferred to a very formidable battery of heavy guns, 9.2 inch calibre at Cape Banks, the northern head of Botany Bay.

We are Moved North

After the Coral Sea naval victory the immediate danger of attack on the east coast was removed and we were re-equipped and sent north. We considered ourselves seasoned soldiers by then. Although we had not seen action we were now adequately trained and equipped. Our boyishness had given place to a maturity I now realize was beyond our years and had been conditioned by the strict discipline of army life.

Troops sent to New Guinea wore 'jungle greens' whereas we were issued with khaki tropical uniforms. We knew Darwin would be our destination but did not expect to be told and what's more encouraged, to draw as much attention to ourselves as possible. But this is what happened. We also went up via Queensland — the normal route for troops going to New Guinea. Our movement was, we discovered, to be an Intelligence ploy to confuse the enemy and maybe give the impression that we were the beginning of a build-up for an attack on Timor. We were also told that the camp we were going to in Darwin had been wiped out in a Jap air attack with heavy loss of life. When we finally arrived, after 14 days' overland journey by train and lorry, we found that bombs had indeed fallen right through the camp but by some miracle had not damaged anything important and no one had been injured or killed. The rumour of serious damage was another Intelligence ploy.

The War Ends

I spent the rest of the war years in Darwin prepared and waiting for a Jap invasion which never came but which we were always led to believe was imminent.

We knew that even if Japan lost the war their troops in the islands just north of us would probably not surrender and we would have to go in after them. The atomic bombs dropped on Hiroshima and Nagasaki altered this scenario entirely and at the age of 23 I found myself in a world at peace once more.

Japanese POWs were brought from Timor to construct a compound for those Japanese arrested for war crimes such as cruelty, etc. The trial was to take place in Darwin as soon as all preparations were made. We had the opportunity of seeing at close quarters our erstwhile enemy and we were impressed. Their Captain was a tall athletic man who spoke English perfectly. He was educated in England and was no doubt hand-picked for the job of leading his men, who were all good physical specimens too and communicating with our officers without being disadvantaged. This paid off on one occasion when an ugly incident could have easily got out of hand.

We had erected fish traps in the harbour from which we augmented our otherwise plain diet and gave us the means of bartering with other units stationed inland.

A Sergeant gave a group POWs permission to take some fish from the traps at low tide but he failed to tell anyone about it. When our men went to empty the traps they saw red and attacked the 'interlopers'. There was an enquiry of course and the matter was resolved with apologies all round, thanks to good communication and diplomacy.

I regained my civilian status on 4 July 1946. We all had degrees of difficulty adjusting to our new roles after nearly 5 years of army regimentation. We had changed but so too had those at home. Many of the values we had known were gone or changed for ever and we had to adapt to post-war society.

The relief of surviving such a terrible period of history still lingers with those who remember.

Very few of us have much say in living our lives as we wish. During the 1939/45 World War I was very much like a grain of sand subject to a stormy sea.

My memories are of forces and events over which I had no control which carried me along and finally cast me back to take my place as best I could.

My 'memoirs' are not spectacular but may be of some interest if seen against the backdrop of the world-shattering drama of those troubled times.

The War Years in Germany

by Lydia White

I was eight years old in 1940, too young some might say to remember much, but not so. At the time we lived in the part of Germany which became East Germany after the war. My father, an aircraft engineer, had found work in the region in 1935 and my mother with my elder sister and myself had followed in 1938 from Bottrop, West Germany. Father had first found two rooms in an old, large house in a small village in which the four of us lived for a year. In 1939 we moved to a small gatekeeper's cottage on the outskirts of Stassfurt. The setting was beautiful but this did not compensate for the lack of plumbing. There was no indoor toilet and water had to be drawn from a tap some 50 metres away. My mother had given birth to another baby girl in the winter, the weather was bitterly cold and the water often frozen. At the beginning of 1940 conditions in the cottage were totally unsuitable for a new-born baby and my parents had decided to let a young childless couple foster the baby. I shall never forget my mother's anguish and the way she suffered from the separation, although she tried to hide it from Father. We tried to console each other and we often cried together. Later we moved again and this time to a modern, large and very comfortable flat in which we lived until 1946.

We lived in Stassfurt, a town about 40 km east of Magdeburg. The suffix -furt means ford and in ancient times the river Bode was crossed on foot or by cart. Founded over a thousand years ago the town naturally had many historical features and Father never seemed to tire of pointing out things and rendering explanations as we wandered on — something he did until he died. I remember, for example, first learning in this way something about the differences and distinctions between Gothic and Roman architecture and comparisons being drawn with recent building styles and materials. I found his way of initiating us into history far more interesting than the abstract textbook method used by my teachers, and it is something I bear in mind when standing in the classroom myself now. I don't remember how many inhabitants lived in the town at that time but I do remember modern estates being built, which were obviously much needed judging by our own experience. It was an important agricultural area and as such was never under-estimated. The rich soil always seemed to yield a good harvest. Near

127

by was a salt mine which we visited and which left a lasting impression. Recent information published by the East German government reveals that Stassfurt now has a population of 26,000 and that it is the only town in the country in which television receivers are manufactured. The information quotes that the county is noted for its industrial and agricultural contributions towards the economy of East Germany.

School life did not start until I was six years old and young children only had to attend for about two hours in the morning, this was gradually extended but I was always home by lunch-time. There was no public transport and it took at least thirty minutes to walk to school in all weathers, and then of course I had to walk back. Books were carried in a leather bag on our backs which left our hands free. There was no such thing as obtaining books or any kind of equipment needed for lessons from the school; parents had to pay for and provide everything. The curriculum in my school was extremely basic at that age and consisted of much learning by rote, German and arithmetic basically. Arithmetic lessons centred around the four rules of number and there were no provisions for practical or experimental work such as children experience in their primary schools now to develop a conceptual understanding of the principles involved. Language work included reading, and handwriting exercises which were tedious and repetitious. Everybody had to write in the same way with letters leaning to the right and absolutely everyone had to write with their right hand. My sister who was naturally left-handed spent many unhappy hours practising, especially the slant to the right. We had to write stories — mainly for homework and I think it was probably during that year that I had to write a story called 'The Adventure of the Lost Penny.' Twenty-five years later my son wrote practically the same story in another country and another language, and only a few weeks ago a neighbour's daughter was set the same exercise by her teacher in the local village school!

Mother always had to sign homework and under any comments a teacher made in one's books. There were no extra curricular activities of any kind and I only remember one class outing during a morning. We collected leaves and I couldn't work out what I was supposed to do with them. Art and craft work did not exist either although I had needlework once a week. That year it was knitting and I started a pair of baby socks of which I never completed the first one. I received the lowest mark of my whole school career and Mother referred to this quite frequently, deploring the fact as in her eyes it was most definitely an asset to be adept at needlework. I was to disappoint her on that score for years to come. Our sporting activities generally took place on a Saturday morning but for young children there was no great emphasis on any particular aspect of physical education. I cannot remember whether the fact that Germany was at war already had an effect or not at that time on our schooling.

Every day when coming home from school I had to do my homework first, this was part of the school day but there was plenty of time in the afternoons and evenings to go out and play.

As soon as the weather permitted I went swimming, a sport which I pursued passionately. Children were eligible for season tickets to the local outdoor swimming pools which were set into a lake. This lake was said to be a caved in salt mine, and certainly the water was as salty as any ocean I have been in.

The games we played were in a seasonal cycle, much as can be observed now. One popular game among young children was spinning tops. The tops were made from wood and varied in size and diameter. A straight rod or stick with string attached to the end was the second piece of equipment needed. The end of the string was evenly wound around the top. The conically shaped top was held gently, point downwards, on the ground. A quick pull on the stick unrolled the top and started it spinning. The winner was the child who managed to keep his top spinning longest by whipping it with the string. I had a large collection of different spinning tops which I cherished. It was of course a game which involved parents in little expense.

Another game we played was a variation of rounders, and of course we also invented many ball games, making up our own rules. Looking back one realizes that most of our group activities were extremely energy-consuming, a fact which has not changed for children.

On sunny summer weekends we went sailing as my Father had bought a sailing dinghy. We sailed on lakes and rivers like the Bode, Saale and even the Elbe. The latter had heavy river traffic and I was frightened more than once by the sight of huge cargo boats passing us in either direction. My Mother used flatly to refuse Father's attempt to persuade her to come sailing and used my baby sister as an excuse not to step into the boat. We would camp on sites by the river or lake and supper was literally cooked on open camp fires. Adults would sit around it for hours. It was not unusual for someone to play the guitar and accordion and Father to join in with playing his mouth-organ until late into the night.

It seemed on the whole a tranquil year and the concept of war and strife between nations was beyond my comprehension at the age of eight. I do not remember anything happening in my narrow world at that time which would have helped me gain an understanding of what was happening outside it with, perhaps, one exception. It must have been in the autumn of 1940 because my baby sister was now home again and I was allowed to take her out in the pram. On this particular day people had started to gather by the roadside and the crowd began to swell. The sound of drums and trumpets became audible and a military band appeared on foot, followed by marching soldiers. There was also a mounted regiment — I had never seen such an impressive sight. The parade included military equipment pulled by lorries. It was a very, very long parade or so it appeared to me. I was on the opposite side of the road from my home and I must have decided that I had had enough because when I saw a space which seemed to give me sufficient room to get through I made a dash for the other side of the road. I can hear the gasps of the crowd now. I might add that the parade continued to ground on relentlessly and at the same pace. Later when it was all over I received a severe slap on my backside from Father, one of the very few he administered to us children.

We had no shortages of food that I was aware of and there was plenty of fresh fruit, with the exception of course of oranges and bananas, but then I did not know what they were and therefore did not miss them.

We were a close and happy family and my parents obviously wanted it that way but the traumas and heartaches were soon to come and last for many years.

Towards the end of 1940 my life centred around the family and when we were told that Mother was expecting another baby my parents hoped that the fourth would turn out to be a boy, but on February 6th 1941, on my father's 38th birthday, my mother presented him with his fourth daughter, Monika. Father was delighted and came home from the hospital telling me that now I would have a baby to take care of too. I had been jealous of my elder sister Margot who, in my eyes, had been favoured because she was allowed to help take care of Helga, and it was obvious that Helga responded much more to Margot. The two have remained close but to this day so have my youngest sister and I. I loved the very close contact with the baby and learned much from it.

I was almost oblivious of anything else. The fact that a war was raging in the outside world did not cloud my days and had little meaning. Outwardly the year and also the following year were similar in pattern. But life had begun to change. Father had less and less time for us. For example a weekly treat which was spending the early part of Sunday mornings in bed with him while Mother was busy preparing breakfast gradually ceased. The four of us used to crowd into the large double bed begging him to tell us about his latest 'dream', and out would come the most fantastic and often hilarious stories. My favourite was the 'recurring' dream about Jumbo the elephant which always arrived by parachute — an umbrella, held with his trunk — just in time to rescue little children. My young sisters used to cuddle up to him or sit spellbound, depending on the story. Once when I questioned the feasibility of this, and got Mother's umbrella to demonstrate the impossibility by jumping off the edge of the bed with the opened umbrella, I received a 'lecture' on lift-off techniques and air currents. He also drew a series of sketches to illustrate Jumbo's adventures.

I had learnt to play chess before I was old enough to go to school, literally while sitting on my father's knees while he played with friends, and over the years it had become a habit on long winter evenings for the two of us to play regularly and on many occasions I played games with his friends. Evenings like these and early Sunday morning 'dreams' gradually became rarer as Father started to return home later, working over the weekend or being absent for several days. This had an unsettling and upsetting effect on all of us. My father became more serious and laughter was less spontaneous. When he was at home he spent more and more time in his room over his drawing-board. He worked for Junkers Aircraft and in retrospect it is easy to work out why, when one looks at the chronicled facts of the war, because aircraft such as the JU 88 were suffering heavy casualties at the hands of the Allied forces. All this though was not known to me at the time. We had a radio, of course, but this was in Father's study and not very often switched on when I was sitting in one of his armchairs to read quietly or do my homework.

Neither of my parents discussed the war with us children until towards the end. My father said later, when he related some of the ordeals he had lived through during the First World War, that he would have done anything to spare us the experience of war.

News was now arriving that several close relatives had been bombed out. They lived in and around Bottrop, where I had been born, just a few miles from Essen where part of the Krupp empire was situated. In fact it was in the heart of Germany's industrial region of the Ruhr/Rheinland. My parents, my elder sister and myself set off to visit them, and I had been excited at the prospect of the journey as I always loved travelling. But a great shock lay in store for us. Seeing the devastation and the ruins of houses and homes I had been so familiar with was immense. The visit was also my introduction to air raids. The first time I heard them the sirens struck terror in my heart and they still do. The sound of the sirens was followed by waves of aircraft dropping bombs all around us. We survived, bodily unhurt, but shaken to the core. I hoped, like children do, that I would wake up and find it had been a nightmare but of course it wasn't. It was only the beginning of the disappearance of sanity from my life.

After experiences like this I became more conscious of the world around me. I became aware of and took more notice of the propaganda posters in the streets and on corners exclaiming the dangers of the 'enemy', what would happen to us if we did not win the battle for our Fatherland which the Führer was leading, and so on. At school we learnt and sang songs about it which were designed to stir in us a greater sense of patriotism. There are probably few children in the world who would not respond positively to their elders in authority when exposed systematically and continually over a period of time to propaganda. Only of course they don't call it propaganda. Children are very susceptical to indroctrination, especially when surrounded by the reality of bombing and men being called up for service and not returning home because they have been killed. I began to believe that we were locked in a struggle for our very survival, but at that age it did not occur to me to question the causes and reasons for it all.

The patriotic songs were a very small part of school life. My teachers were strict and all learning was taken very seriously. Looking back I realize that in literature for example we covered much more in the German classics than one would suppose. We performed some of them as plays with Goethe's *Faust* standing out particularly. I also shed my first tears during a performance of Shakespeare's *Romeo and Juliet*, which I had already read. Victor Hugo's *Les Miserables* was also on the syllabus. In a school curriculum cut down to the bare bone, the cultural aspects were nevertheless seen as important. We were taught areas in mathematics such as geometry, algebra and fractions at the age of ten which I would not attempt to teach to the majority of twelve-year-olds in the abstract. Much of it was certainly learning by rote and you either understood what you were taught or you didn't. One was moved up or down in the class according to one's standard of work compared with the rest of the class. On this principle children were often moved within their classes for any subject and someone always had to be number 35 or whatever the lowest number in the class was. It was a real stigma to be at the lower end and I have been taught by some very insensitive teachers who were not above referring to a child as stupid.

Corporal punishment was freely adminstered very often, and in this there was 'equality' between the sexes. The gulf between teachers and children was never bridged in my experience and I was very frightened of my mathematics teacher. Children who did not achieve the required grades had to repeat the year, a practice which continues to this day in Germany. The psychology of learning and its bearing on education was most likely either a luxury or unknown to most of the teachers I came in contact with. However, to be fair, the stress of teaching under war-time conditions could have been the cause, but it had a profound effect on me and influenced me much later, when in 1971, I decided to become a teacher in this country and studied at a London University teacher training college.

By 1943/44 our attendances at school became erratic, not by choice, but by force. On many occasions classes were taken from all the schools in town to work in the fields. Trailers were hitched behind tractors or lorries every day for a whole week (including Saturdays) to harvest whatever needed harvesting. Carrots, cabbages, potatoes — the list is endless. I hated, but absolutely and utterly hated, every single moment I spent in one of those fields, which seemed to stretch far beyond the horizon. I resented getting dirty and wet and cold or being without any shade or shelter. The migraines from which I suffered increased in frequency and I was often sick and blacked out. There was little sympathy from the staff either, who probably preferred a classroom to the fields too, but I never heard any of them complain. My poor head was no excuse for not being carted off to the fields. God knows my mother tried, with the help of our doctor, to be allowed to keep me home at times but all to no avail. How I loathed the countryside. We were too far out of town to hear any air raid sirens and Allied planes often flew above us across the sky to some bombing mission. We were given the pretty futile instruction to throw ourselves flat on the ground. I wonder if any of the pilots ever gave us a thought as they flew above our heads, sometimes quite low.

During the morning we were each given a thick slice of bread with either margarine or jam and our lunch-time food consisted of thick soup. The main ingredient was always potatoes with either beans or peas added if it was a good day — on a bad day it could be barley added to the potatoes and the taste was truly revolting. At the end of each day we also lined up for our wages — 1 Mark, which I always saved as there was nothing one could spend it on.

At the same time my eldest sister, then aged 15 to 16, was similarly used as slave labour under the disguise of having to be patriotic. She was working long hours in the fields and the house of the farmer where she and other girls had been sent. Unfortunately she was a long way from home and very homesick, her letters were pitiful. I think most young girls had to work like her unless the parents had influence in higher places.

Air raids had become a way of life by 1944 and the cellar ceiling in our house had duly been strengthened with posts, which made me feel more secure — but looking out of my study window now, across our garden, I realize that the posts were little more than psychological props, because they were no thicker than those we are using to build an arbour for our climbing roses.

Apart from cracked walls and broken windows we suffered no personal bomb damage. The worst day-time raid we experienced was aimed at destroying an underground fuel depot which was no further than two or three kilometres from our house. To us children the area was just a disused lignite mine and we often played in the overgrown grounds. There was rolling stock on the railway tracks to which we paid little attention, although we were warned not to play there. The attack on the fuel depot was unexpected. No siren had sounded the alarm and I was playing outside with friends when we heard the sound of the planes; looking up we actually saw the bombs dropping from the planes and we just threw ourselves on the ground and only then did the alarm sound. The following day we heard that a boy and his mother whom we knew had been killed in the raid and sadly several friends and I decided to pay our last respects. We guessed that the bodies had been taken to the chapel in the old cemetery across the road from our house. Looking through the chapel window we expected to see two coffins but found ourselves looking at the two bodies lying on the floor. We were paralysed by the unexpected sight and one child was sick on the spot. We started to run and did not stop until we were out of breath.

Between us we decided not to tell anyone but then I started to suffer from the most horrific nightmares. As soon as I had to go to bed I became terrified and frightened of the dark. I resorted to waking my young sister, telling her stories until we fell asleep from exhaustion. Needless to say my mother found out and for some time she slept with us, especially as my father's absences increased. Because of his work he was among the men who had not been drafted into the forces, but of course all our young male relatives had. One cousin lost his life in the Baltic Sea in the *Gustlow* and two others, brothers aged 21 and 23, were posted missing during the battle of Stalingrad. My aunt died in the early 1960s firmly believing her sons were alive but prisoners in Siberia somewhere.

The winter of 1944/45 was cold. We only had enough fuel to warm one room and, with the exception of potatoes, food was scarce and clothes were getting extremely threadbare. A full night's sleep was rare. I often observed my parents talking quietly alone when my father was at home, but most of all I noticed how utterly tired he looked during the few hours he spent at home. My mother tried hard to make our Christmas a happy one, as a Roman Catholic she naturally cherished this tradition, and we sang around our Christmas tree as usual. My two little sisters seemed unaware of the atmosphere and crisis just as I had been not so long before.

Early in January 1945 my mother told me that she had been informed that I was due for a long promised State holiday, and that I was to be spending a winter break skiing and skating in Thuringa (Thüringer Wald) a very beautiful region south of Weimar. What was it that made parents part with their children as late as February 1945? I thought it was faith in the mysterious weapon I had heard about which would help us to win the war. In the case of my parents, as they told me afterwards, it was faith and hope in sanity, because they were convinced that there would be a surrender to the Allied forces to avoid fighting on German soil, and they thought it would be safer for me to be out of the way during what they thought would be the last attacks from the air. Father had tried to make arrangements for my mother and two younger sisters to stay somewhere safer but did not succeed.

In February I found myself, a large label around my neck bearing my name and address, on the station where a group of children had already assembled. I knew none of them. I was supposed to enjoy the thought of a holiday in the snow and all I could think of through my tears was why had my mother left me so quickly and why couldn't I stay at home?

I don't remember the outward journey but the place where we stayed was lovely. For a few days I had some exhilarating moments. The snow was just right and the natural slopes in good condition. There was no shortage of winter sports equipment and we spent every possible moment outside. The home may well have been a privately owned residence at some time and it was beautiful. There were several dozen children in residence and several of us shared a room. The indoor routine was rigid and run on a tight schedule. We were marched in and out of the dining-rooms like soldiers and the food was almost identical to that dished out to us in the fields during harvesting. There was no seconds and I was often hungry. In the evenings I was very unhappy and withdrawn. I did not take part in games which the adults organized and they simply sent me to bed for being 'sulky'. The temperature and atmosphere was cold and unfamiliar. I felt abandoned and lonely, wondering what life was all about.

I had become aware of the thundering sounds of guns which was something I became more and more frightened of. A few days later we were all called together in a great hurry and asked to put up our hands if we thought we could travel home alone. I have never volunteered for anything so fast in my life again. Shortly afterwards I was in a group of children, each of whom was clutching a bag and a packet of sandwiches, being taken to the station, again with our labels around our necks. Someone put me on the train, third class of course with slatted seats, and it dawned on me that all I knew was that Stassfurt was in a north-westerly direction. But I was quite proud of myself and satisfied. The train had not long been in motion as I sat munching one of my precious sandwiches when, suddenly a man sitting opposite me shot across and pulled me on the floor and under the seat. All around hell seemed to have broken loose. Bombs were hailing down. The train had stopped and I was lying there trying to cover my ears and face. When the sound of the explosions had died down the man asked me if I was all right and my mechanical "Yes" was accepted without question. The man helped me down from the train. There were people crying and moaning and when some of the dust settled large craters became visible. The man who had helped me was gone. People, uninjured like myself, started to walk and I just followed — for how long I don't know. No one spoke to me. People were preoccupied with themselves.

Eventually I found myself on a station with the group I had followed and there we waited. Time was meaningless. Everyone sheltered as best they could, including me. I must have dozed a few times because I became aware of people moving and not realizing that a train had pulled into the station. Whether people were going somewhere or coming back from somewhere, like me, was of no importance. I ended up sitting on the floor of the moving train having just followed the crowd. Again time meant nothing and I have really no idea of how often the train stopped, where or when. I saw someone eating and began to realize that my mouth was dry and that I was hungry, but I did not have the courage to ask anyone for food. There were children on the train but certainly no childish laughter. People were sombre and some babies cried. I found myself looking out of the window. I don't know how long it took me to realize that I was travelling through familiar countryside. I don't know when I realized that the next station would be one I knew (Güsten) but I became excited because this was only about 10km from my home town.

It took some time for me to absorb that the train was not stopping at my station and for the first time I broke down and sobbed. I don't think anyone around me noticed or much cared as I was left alone. The train went on for what seemed eternity and eventually when it stopped I got off and found myself to be the only person who had alighted. A railway guard approached me and asked where I wanted to go and bursting into tears I showed him my label which I had taken off. After a while I found myself with a sandwich in my hands in his office being told not to worry. I am sure I never thanked that guard properly but I was very grateful. A couple of hours later I was put on a train in the guard's van, with the assurance that it would stop at Stassfurt. I should have appreciated that it was a miracle that some of the railway system was still functioning, but I didn't.

When the train stopped at my station I got off and just walked home, wondering what I would find. It is true that the longest mile home is the last mile, only in my case it was a few kilometres. My mother and two youngest sisters were at home and it was joyous to see the disbelief and happiness in her face when she saw me. Again and again she asked me how I had managed to get home. I was scrubbed down and put to bed, for how long I do not know, but according to my mother I slept through several air raids. Just a few days after my return, my eldest sister suddenly appeared in the doorway having made her way home in much the same way as I did, but as she had been in a westerly direction from us she had suffered much more, and a journey of a few hours had taken her a week. She had just walked away from the farm when she realized that the fighting was getting out of hand.

My father, who had been absent, returned home tired and exhausted and for a short time the whole family was under one roof, but we spent much of our time in our air raid shelter. It was March and the day-time raids had increased enormously. There was comfort in all of us being together but nothing seemed 'normal', indeed I could not remember anything but being frightened during bombing raids, hearing about yet another cousin being killed and relatives being bombed out. At the beginning of April, five weeks before the war ended for us, the biggest bombshell for my mother fell on us — my father was being called up, and within two days he was gone. He had told us that we were to help Mother, showed both my eldest sister and myself in the presence of my mother where our little safe was and the most important papers concerning bank accounts and registration certificates and so on, and told us that as the war was in the last stages, Hitler was bound to surrender any moment, and that he would be back very quickly. My mother was devastated. My father was the undisputed head of the household and I am sure that it was he who had made most of the important decisions in the past, or at least had the final word, and my mother was sure that she would not see him again. One need only read the propaganda of those last few turbulent weeks before the war ended to know that everyone was expected to fight to the last drop of blood.

School continued but everything was often interrupted by air raids. At all other times my mother insisted that we must be near the house and she did most of the shopping herself. I knew how much she suffered for we had not heard anything of my father, and after all she was left with four children to take care of. Somehow the weeks went by until on the 7th May 1945 (dates are indelibly imprinted upon my mind) a vehicle toured the streets informing all inhabitants that if, or when, the sirens sounded for five minutes uninterrupted, it would mean that the enemy had entered the outskirts of our town and that everyone should stay indoors. For some time we had been aware that the fighting was getting nearer and nearer and for days now my mother had refused to let me attend school, but she insisted that I worked and she checked that I did, so did my eldest sister, in fact she quite bullied me and I felt unfairly treated.

It was early morning, May 8th, that I became aware that the sirens were wailing away but did not stop, the sound just went on and on. I can hardly believe that it only lasted for five minutes because the sound just seemed to engulf me and suddenly I felt weak in the knees. This was it! It may be our last day on earth! I was convinced that what I had heard would come true, which was that everyone would be put against the nearest wall and shot. My sister was equally sure, and both she and my mother looked terrible. My mother was literally clutching my two little sisters. No one spoke a word and the silence was only broken when I heard my mother say, "Come away from the window"! I had been looking out wondering what would happen next and no doubt this thought passed through many people's minds at the same time. I saw several youths, dressed in Hitler Youth uniform, with grenades and other weapons cross the green in front of our house and disappear down the unmade road by the side of it, then a tank appeared on the main road. It was moving at walking pace with soldiers by its side ready to fire. My mother pulled us away from the window and we remained at the farthest end of the room for some time. Shooting started and stopped again and we gradually made our way to the window again.

The main street was crowded with tanks, vehicles, and soldiers who had started to come down the side street towards us. My heart beat so fast and loud that I was sure it could be heard outside. I genuinely thought that now our last moments had arrived and I prayed that it would be quick and vaguely reflected what it might be like. The suspense was terrible. The spell was broken by a voice shouting through the loudspeaker that everyone who was not harbouring anybody connected with the military services was to hang a white flag from their window. This command was repeated many times and my mother obeyed by hanging a white table-cloth from one of our windows. A further instruction was that everybody had to remain in their homes. I am not sure how long this first curfew lasted but eventually everyone was visited by a group of soldiers making house to house calls. My mother spoke to them alone and when we asked what they wanted, she told us that the soldiers were trying to establish how many people lived in each place and where any absent members of the family were. Mother had been able to say in all sincerity that she did not know where my father was and had in fact broken down because she thought he must be dead. Later she confided that she had considered turning on the gas with all of us in one room, as she could not imagine any future at all, and it was only her faith, which of course condemns this, which prevented her from going through with it.

Considering the relatively sheltered life my mother had led she coped very well with the situation, and I like to think that we children helped, each in our own way.

It had been the American forces who had reached us first and my mother found out that, apart from the Hitler Youths who had, according to her information, refused to stop and surrender, there had been no loss of life in the town. Adults were allowed to go out for one hour in the morning and one hour in the afternoon and this was extended later to two hours. Children had to stay at home. Gradually the curfew was lifted but of course there was no school, which meant doing homework supervised by my mother and sister. I realized much later that my mother was trying to keep some kind of routine going, but the odds were too much against it.

Unbeknown to us my father, with other older new recruits, had been sent to the 'front', which was at that time already east of the Rhine. According to him they arrived near Paderborn and were almost immediately chased by the American Army, which was equipped with superior weapons and vehicles. The jeeps' versatility in reverse was something that particularly impressed my father. Whatever outfit he was with was very quickly driven back towards the river Weser, and rather than being captured, my father and several other soldiers decided to try and swim across. It was April and freezing and the river was a fast flowing one. The men had jumped in fully dressed and my father almost immediately pulled off all his clothes down to his underpants. Another soldier and he made it to the other side, but my father was sure that several of them were drowned. The two of them made it to the nearest farmhouse and managed to persuade the farmer to let them have some clothes. They were now 'civilians', their clothes and papers being somewhere at the bottom of the river. Of course, officially it must mean they were deserters. The two men split up and after spending a night in the barn my father set off for home. The Americans overtook him very quickly and it was his good English which helped him through. Who knows what sort of and how many lies he told on the way. He later said he regretted one thing, and that was that he had 'borrowed' an unattended bicycle. When he took it he made a note of the place and said that he thought he would be able to do something about it at a later date, but of course as life turned out it was impossible, but he did not forget the incident.

My father arrived home some days after the Americans had entered our town and the war in Europe was over. At first I did not know about it but I should have, because my mother was a different person. She was smiling somehow but secretive. Anyway a day after his return a neighbour said to me, "I hear your father is home," and I asked my mother outright. She took me down to the cellar, which was still fitted out with the bunks for use during night-time air raids, and there was my father, very ill. He had lost an unbelievable amount of weight and vomited a lot, but my mother was just happy that he was home. Now she became extremely worried. Obviously someone had seen him coming home. It was not very long afterwards that a jeep stopped outside our house — some conscientious soul had reported that my father was there. I was sent upstairs and sometime later I saw my father being taken to the jeep and driven away. I had seen him just once. My mother was crying but told us that my father had said that he had been told that he only needed to go along to register, and that he would be released soon and be back home before long. As the hours passed my mother became more and more agitated. She took my father's warm jacket and cycled to the town hall where she was just in time to see him and a number of other men being put on a lorry. She held out the jacket and an American soldier took it from her and threw it on to the lorry just before it drove off. Father picked it up and waved and that was it.

My mother went every day to enquire where he had been taken and she never gave up. The day-time curfew had been lifted and the trips to the town hall became regular pilgrimages. The day came when she said she thought she knew where he was being held. My eldest sister and I were instructed to take care of the two young ones and Mother packed as many odds and ends of food she could manage to amass, and set off with not a hint of exactly where she was heading, saying that what we didn't know we couldn't tell in case we were questioned. She was away a day and a half and when we saw her arrive back she was barely able to walk. Her feet were badly blistered and even bleeding. Altogether she had walked 40 kilometres having traded the bicycle in for more food. It is difficult to believe but she did find the prisoners' camp and through the fence she managed to get someone to look for my father — in exchange for food — and she waited for some hours at the fence. Her faith in herself and human nature was rewarded. How I wish I could have seen them meet. One on either side of the fence, hardly believing their own eyes. They never spoke about it in subsequent years because of course other problems overtook those. What must have gone through their minds as they parted?

We took care of Mother and her feet and made her rest as much as possible. She would not speak about the experience other than telling us that she had seen him and the camp was in the direction of Magdeburg. A week later she set off again, on foot, and she actually made that trip four or five times, swearing us to secrecy. How can one describe such love and devotion in words?

It was summer and people were beginning to laugh again at certain things and, dare I say it, even plan for the future. We, in our ignorance, even hoped that Father would be home soon and life could start afresh. What a good thing it is that we cannot look into the future, for had I known what was ahead I would have played less happily with my sisters and friends. We had forgotten what life without air raids had been like and we were enjoying the usual games children play. There was no school of course and I began to feel uneasy about it.

We saw a lot of the armed forces but I never had any close contact. The American soldiers always seemed to be driving around in their jeeps and seemed to talk and laugh at anything. It did not occur to me that they might be just as happy and relieved that the fighting was over. In the neighbourhood various people were becoming very friendly with the soldiers and pretty girls started to go out with the Americans. My seventeen-year-old sister kept herself aloof. She scoffed at the girls who went out with American soldiers but they probably had not seen their fathers taken away from them. It was still all unreal because their fathers were usually away too, there were in fact very few men around, and those who were at home were either young teenagers or old men. On the whole though life had calmed down a lot, then one morning in August we woke up and looking out of the window across the green in front of the house I saw, as far as the eye could see, a mass of dirty shaven heads, which were attached to equally dirty bodies and clothes to match. I can see them now and I am probably totally incapable of being objective about it. The Russians had arrived! I did not even know of the power struggle that was going on between the Allies. I also had little understanding of what it could mean to us. For three days our town was occupied by both the American Army and the Russian Army. It is, for me, a sad fact that the American Army withdrew beyond the river Elbe. Immediately another curfew was imposed. Only adults were allowed to go out twice a day for one hour, which was later extended to 2 hours. Eventually the curfew was lifted during the day, but life under the Russians was very different from life under the Americans. Still no school, of course, and the whole atmosphere seemed oppressed. It began to dawn on me what a different race the Americans must be. To me they had appeared a happy-go-lucky type of people, but the Russian soldiers were very different. To me they gave the impression of being ignorant peasants but I did say that I was unable to be objective about them. Not so the Russian officers, and I did meet several on a number of occasions. Not long after the Russians arrived they started to dismantle the aircraft factory where my father had worked, they also started to visit the homes of people who had worked there and of course they also came to us. My mother and my sister and myself were questioned many times about my father and asked where he was. We could answer honestly that we did not know where he was. We received visits for some time and I know that on several occasions my sister and also my mother were required to drink Vodka — neat, just like the Russians drank it, but they really did not know where my father was therefore the visits proved negative from the Russian point of view, but my mother became more and more agitated and worried.

Certain dates stand out in my memory like a sore thumb and it was December 21st 1945 when my mother told us that we would be "leaving and returning to where we came from." She made us dress in several sets of clothes, my eldest sister and I also had a big bag to carry as had my mother. It may be difficult to imagine but I did not question it. I remember we made our way to the station and waited but after a time my mother said we would just go to ---- and I can't remember the name. In fact we walked in the direction of Magdeburg. It was so very cold. At one station we managed to get on a train and we ended up in Magdeburg. There I remember we crossed the Elbe on foot, having had to get off the train. I just followed my mother and, I am sure, so did my eldest sister. That night we spent in a doorway in a place I can't remember. We were huddled together and I think exhaustion must have had something to do with our getting some sleep. At day-break my mother asked me to go to a farm which was close by to see if they could spare a hot drink. The lady who answered the door told me in not a very polite tone of voice that they did not have anything to spare. It was a rejection that was hard to bear. It had been my first attempt at begging and my two young sisters were badly in need of something and so were the rest of us. My mother just said that it was time we were on our way and on our way we went.

We walked and walked. We hit on the idea of putting each of my little sisters in the big bag in turn. Helga would be carried from one telegraph post to the next and then Monika and so we went from village to village. In between we knocked on various doors to ask if they had any 'Ersatz' coffee to spare but every time the answer was that the people did not even have enough for themselves. We were down to a bag of biscuits and for the remainder of the day my sister and myself had three biscuits each. I am sure that my mother did not have any. That night we crawled into a barn without asking permission. It was like a haven and I would have been quite happy to stay forever. It was warm in comparison with the icy world outside and I did not feel inclined to move the next morning, but my mother managed to rouse us and we continued our trek. Progress was slow which is not difficult to imagine, after all we had a five-and a six-year-old child with us. The children rarely complained.

The road we were on led us to a small town where we joined a major road. There we realized that a number of people were making their way in the same direction as we were, that is towards the west. Someone with a handcart allowed my little sisters to sit on top which relieved us from carrying them, and we pulled the cart instead. By then I know I felt extremely exhausted and I sat down for a moment by the side of the road. I did not feel particularly cold or anything and I could not understand why my mother was getting angry and shouting at me to get up, all I wanted was to rest and I told her I would catch up with her. This made her more angry and she pulled me up. She realized the danger of my condition, but I had not. We carried on walking and at one stage when I turned round I noticed that there were hundreds of people behind us. The column was moving slowly but surely in the same direction as ourselves. We joined a stream of refugees. Most of them carried bags on their backs and in their hands and children too had rucksacks — a few lucky ones pulled handcarts or pushed prams with their most precious possessions, just what these were I would like to know. The main aim seemed to be to place one foot in front of the other. Occasionally someone stopped by the wayside. There was little talk between people and I never asked anyone where they had come from or where they were going, neither did I think of asking why they were walking through the snow like us. Thinking was totally beyond me.

Nothing had any meaning. We had a few biscuits left in our linen bag but I don't remember thinking about food either.

We had reached a railway track and for some time were walking beside it until we reached a stationary train. It was full of people but somehow we succeeded in scrambling on and sat on some empty floor space, under a window without glass, which was probably the reason why, for the moment, there was space. There were no seats and most of the windows were broken but it afforded some shelter nevertheless. It was getting dark and some enterprising people had started a fire near the train. Many refugees dragged wood from the nearby copse and a concerted effort by a lot of people resulted in railway sleepers being made 'available' and heaved on top of the fire. It must have been the biggest bonfire of all time. But so low was the temperature that one's front facing the fire became too hot while one's back was still too cold to stand still. People were now talking to each other, relating where they had come from and from the sound of it they had travelled, or rather walked, for weeks, coming from parts which were hundreds of kilometres east of us, but I was not interested. That I remember this much is remarkable. I huddled my sisters inside the train and together we drifted on and off into uneasy catnaps. I did think that it was just possible that I might wake up and find myself back at home surrounded by warm familiar things, finding that I had just had a nightmare. When I did wake up I wished that I hadn't and hoped that perhaps I would sink into a deep sleep from which I would never wake up. I was not yet fourteen years old!

There were some Russian soldiers near by but they did not interfere with life around the train. It was not until much later that I realized that we had been at Helmsted — which is still such an important crossing point between the East and West.

We spent the bitterly cold night on the train and by the following morning there was a visible restlessness among the adults. Rumours were spreading that the train would be allowed to move. I was ignorant of the full implications of this. I only vaguely remembered what life had been like for the short time that we had experienced life under American occupation, and the concept of democracy was unkown to me. At that particular time the Allied forces were stationed about a couple of kilometres away on the other side of the wood, the adults knew this and there was a quiet expectancy in the air which changed to excitement. It was infectious and I too started to wait for something to happen. The train really did start to move but only for a few yards then stopped. This happened frequently during the next few hours and had a bad effect on people. There was much shouting and talking. Eventually late in the afternoon the train set off again at walking pace with Russian soldiers, armed of course, walking alongside the train. So we moved slowly through the wood. Then my eldest sister did something unpredictable and silly. We were looking out of the windowless carriage when Margot stuck her tongue out at the Russian soldiers under the window. Shortly afterwards the train stopped again and we were both convinced that her stupid actions had caused yet another delay. We were very frightened and hiding in a corner by now ready to swear it wasn't her, when the train set off again and gradually it gained speed. There were great shouts of excitement and people were hugging each other.

It was now dark and, of course, there was no light in the train, but the journey was relatively short and when it came to a halt at a small station everyone alighted. We all just lined up and some British soldiers together with Red Cross nurses handed out mugs with steaming liquid in it. I don't remember tasting it — just feeling the warmth down my throat and into my stomach. Then we were in another queue. Someone put some disgusting powder down my front and back and looked into my hair. I felt rebellious against this but we must truly have looked a dirty dishevelled sight. We had not washed for several days, the open countryside was our toilet and we must have smelled accordingly. We were allocated some floor space in a huge barn with straw on the floor and told by my mother not to move, while she joined the queue to register us. As if we could have moved! We sank into the straw and in the considerably warmer conditions I went into a very deep sleep, so deep that my mother had trouble rousing me. Whilst the four of us had been asleep, along with many other people, my mother had not rested. She had, while giving the authorities details about ourselves, also reported my father missing and in those blurred and insane days she was given the first ray of hope. It was just possible that my father was among the prisoners in a camp not very far away, as the Americans had withdrawn with their prisoners, and there was a large concentration of them in the area. A few hours later a miracle occurred — an American Army lorry arrived with a number of men on it, and one was my father. Words are inadequate to describe an experience such as that, and it was the 24 December, 1945. We had been on the road for only three days but it was a lifetime and an experience like that has to be lived through before it can be understood.

The Americans had organized many prisoners into work-gangs and my father, being an engineer, had been going round farms on a programme of repairing farm machinery. Whenever a large group of refugees arrived at Helmsted some of the prisoners went, armed with a list of names, to see if anyone had arrived who could be reunited with a prisoner or family in the West. The Red Cross performed heroic tasks but we had just been truly lucky.

Father had some kind of pass as a 'trusted' prisoner and he managed to get us on the back of the lorry under some blankets. I am sure we all felt that now we could face anything after this particular year which was drawing to a close, and it is merciful that we cannot see into the future because the next five years proved to be very difficult and on occasions there was extreme hardship. But on this Christmas Eve as we were setting off for yet another unknown destination the future only consisted of the immediate needs, which was a roof over our heads. I don't know what I expected as we arrived in a small village called Schöppensted. We waited in the small square while Mother and Father set off to knock on doors to ask whether they had any room to put us up. It took some hours and we had started to feel so cold and ill again. The wind in particular was very sharp and the blankets we had around us were insufficient.

My father returned and said that he had persuaded a farmer to let him have the key to two rooms which were vacant because the farm-worker had been called up and not returned. I said a silent prayer. We only had to go around the corner through a main entrance door into a courtyard. The rooms could only be reached through the washhouse and were directly above two pigsties and the outdoor toilet, but we did not know that yet. The furniture consisted of two bunk beds with hay bundles in one room and a large box in the second. There was a small stove but no fuel. My parents told us to lie down and none of us objected. The following morning, Christmas Day, we woke up to find a warm fire in what was going to be our kitchen/sitting-room for the next 18 months. There was a white cloth of some kind on the box with some bread and jam and in the corner stood a small Christmas tree, several smaller boxes served as stools.

My father had to report regularly for some time and continued to work repairing machinery, but hardly a day went by with him coming home empty-handed. An old settee appeared to double as a bed for my parents. It was extremely narrow but I wonder if they minded. We gradually acquired a table and chairs, some blankets but no mattresses. Sleeping on hay is not something that I would now do voluntarily. We had a plate each and odd cutlery. Every day we would have to go into the woods surrounding the village to bring home firewood on a sledge borrowed from the other children who shared our courtyard. Our world was very narrow for that short time. We lived from day to day trying to keep warm and live on what food my parents could provide for us. Our staple diet was soup which can be made out of anything, but primarily it consisted of water at first and potatoes second.

As the weather improved my parents sent me to school. My younger sisters were too young and my older sister was too old for the village school which was very small, two classrooms to be precise. One classroom was for the six to ten-year-olds and the other for the ten plus to fourteen-year-olds. The school-leaving age was fourteen. For me the school meant only a few months more, but the headteacher sent a letter to my parents saying there was no real advantage in keeping me there as I had reached a standard way beyond that which was being taught. I can just imagine what an English parent would say in the present day if they received a note like that. In the event I was gradually given the responsibility of looking after the younger class, albeit only checking that they did the work set by the teacher. I started to think that it would be lovely to become a teacher and I started to nurse secret dreams, but they received no nourishment. When I had my birthday I duly left school, feeling totally inadequate. We may have lived in an agricultural area but food was the most important factor in our lives, or rather how to get hold of it.

My mother told me that the local doctor needed help in the house, his wife had one child and could not manage! Helping with the housework and her little boy would entitle me to two meals a day and a few pence a week pocket-money which of course was handed to my mother to help with the food bills. My eldest sister was similarly employed. The resentment I felt was indescribable. Why, I asked myself, should I be cleaning somebody else's floors when my mother used to have someone doing it for her? During the year 1946 I became very much aware of the fact that the farmers and the gentry in the village were living in a style of luxury almost as if there had been no war at all. Their children did not mix with us and did not attend the local school. Refugees like us were treated as second class citizens. Apart from other refugees and the children of some farm workers we had no one to play with and we were outcasts. I realized too that where we were living mattered. During the warmer weather the stench from the pigs and the toilets over which we lived seemed unbearable. We continued to live under these conditions until 1947. My father had been released and no longer had to report to the authorities. After visiting the Rhine/Ruhrland he came back to Schöppensted with the plan of returning there permanently. It was where my eldest sister and I were born.

My parents must have discussed the matter and when my father announced that he would be looking for work in the 'west' and I could go with him to look for somewhere to live I felt elated. Nothing could be worse than being a maid to a doctor's lazy wife.

We arrived in the 'west' staying with relatives who could ill afford another mouth to feed until my father found work at the Chemische Werke Hüls. This is, to the present day, an enormous chemical factory, built up again after the war, I believe, under the 'Marshall Aid Plan'. The work force was more than 20,000 and those men in the same position as my father slept in 'men only' camps. Some weeks later Father collected me from my cousin, saying he had found a possible place to live. The chemical factory encompassed several square kilometres and I was taken, by borrowed bicycle, to the north side of the factory which itself is several km from the town, to an air raid bunker approx 2m × 12m. It had two entrances, no windows, and was built half underground and completely covered with soil above ground. There were some odd pieces of timber which we placed above the least wet patches on the floor and we slept like that for several nights, while during the day my father and I started to dig above ground where he had worked out the future windows would be. I could not imagine them — the walls were half a metre thick but this did not deter my father. We managed to dig away the soil during the next few weeks and I carry the scars in the palms of my hands to this very day. Father managed to break through the walls in two places and set about making window frames and also doors for the two openings. Constructing a toilet on the outside back wall was next. During the day I was on my own and I spent my time digging away. It was a lonely spot. The nearest water tap was over five minutes' walk away and I carried every drop we needed. Again Father gradually managed to acquire certain useful items for the household with never a word of how and where they had come from. A standard phrase was, "What you don't know you cannot tell."

Towards the end of the summer Mother and my three sisters came to join us and we were a family once more. During the last few months in Schöppensted the relationship between my parents and myself had deteriorated. I was very resentful at having to be a housemaid for my food at an age when I thought I should be learning and playing and I really started to feel inferior. My eldest sister too felt that way and my parents being preoccupied with the daily struggle of providing for us had no understanding of our needs as teenagers. During the summer months spent with Father digging I was feeling relatively at peace, if somewhat in a vacuum. Now that we were all together again after the initial feeling of pleasure that the separation was over things between myself and my parents started to go sour again. We were destitute financially and no matter what my parents tried they were unable to draw on our not unsubstantial resources in East Germany. It seems inconceivable now but since the end of the war we did not have a radio nor see a newspaper. I was not ill-informed at 15 in 1947 but totally uninformed. I had no, absolutely no, idea of what was going on in the world and my ignorance was complete. We lived in such an isolated spot that any communication with the outside world and shopping for food was a major problem.

It was during that winter that my father came home telling me that he had heard that there were a few vacancies for assistants to laboratory assistants and I applied, being fortunate to pass the medical examination. I had the body of a present-day underdeveloped 10-year-old. For the next two years I was very happy during the day. I was in a small lab, with one qualified assistant and another girl like myself under the direct auspices of Dr Ahrens, an elderly academic, whose life was chemistry! After a short time he took me under his wing. Slowly he set up experiments for me and gradually he let me take more and more responsibility for, what I am sure were, minor experiments. He was directly concerned with making latex more pliable. Plastic was in its infancy and still very brittle and there was much research into the problem at the time. After about 18 months Dr Ahrens was discussing the necessity for me to start studying seriously and continue my schooling. At home the idea was viewed with dismay. There was no money, grants were unheard of and you couldn't eat chemistry! The quest for food was obsessive and yet there was never quite enough of it. I don't think I ever felt completely satisfied. During the day I worked in an intellectually stimulating environment and I felt I was making a worthwhile contribution. My self-esteem had risen but at home my mother criticized me and continually told me that I should be looking for an apprenticeship of some sort. Hairdressing was one idea put to me. I really could not cope well with these suggestions and I was accused of being big-headed, unrealistic and, most hurtful of all, of relying on others to feed me.

In 1949 when I was not quite 18, and had been working for Dr Ahrens for almost 2 years, my parents increased the pressure, saying that they had heard that the factory was dismissing a large number of its work force, especially those working without qualifications. My mother told me that in town there was a vacancy in a restaurant. There would be a small wage and most important of all full board. She told me that I had to take it, and the following day my father saw Dr Ahrens and told him that I would be leaving, as they could no longer afford to keep me. Dr Ahrens told me how sorry he was and asked me to keep in touch. The job I was now forced into was again housemaid to the restaurant owner's wife — a large, fat, and very arrogant lady who did not even have to try to make one feel inadequate. My resentment grew and my attitude was appalling. Her two young boys treated me as their personal servant and I gritted my teeth more than once and tried to ignore my position. In me grew a determination to believe that there had to be more to life than this. After a few months I refused point blank one morning to go to work. I used to cycle, which took about a half-hour, and I had to start at seven in the morning. My mother could not believe what she heard and there was a great scene. In the end she tried to persuade me to work out a month's notice but I refused. The scene was repeated in the evening when my father came home from work, and what we said to each other was so upsetting that it is difficult to repeat it. I now tried to get my position in the lab back but I failed the medical twice and joined the unemployed.

Hardly a day went by when this was not a subject for discussion. I tried by helping with the vegetable patch and taking care of the various animals we had for different purposes, that was not enough though to stop me from feeling sullen, unhappy and degraded generally. But not everything was a disaster, there were moments of carefree happiness too for a while.

Two girls only a couple of years older than myself lived near by and inevitably we became friends. They were refugees too and in exactly the same situation as ourselves. We had made friends with some young men and I had been going out with my boy-friend for nearly two years. In warm weather we all used to go swimming in the canal, no more than two minutes from us, and we often used to sit on its banks — the young men with their piano accordion and guitars, and we would play and sing which was well within earshot of my parents, who therefore did not object too much. This kind of entertainment cost nothing and was therefore encouraged, especially as I could take care of my two sisters at the same time. The problems started when we attended the occasional dances. I had to ask for the one mark it cost to get in and this I did not get very often. The dances finished at midnight but at eleven my father would stand in the door and tell whoever was near to go and fetch me even if I was in the middle of dancing. Our group would then leave together, walking behind my father. When my 18th birthday approached my boy-friend, who was 20, asked me to become engaged and he spoke to my father who told him in no uncertain terms that I was much too young and that we must wait. Such was the power parents, or my parents, had over their children. Naturally my boy-friend was upset. Slowly at first but steadily the relationship deteriorated between us, as he now refused to come and see me at home, and I was not always allowed out in the evening. One day he told me that he had started to go out with another girl. I was desolate. I loved his smile and enjoyed listening to him playing the accordion. Being so unhappy with other aspects of life he had been my anchor, but I was now adrift.

I very seriously started to think about my future — I had heard that girls were going abroad for two years, especially to England, and I decided to discuss the possibility with my parents. I had silently braced myself for a storm but it did not come. My father sat down very calmly, encouraging me to make enquries, and helping me to formulate my ideas. It took several months to get the necessary paperwork organized and during this time my relationship with my parents improved. My father was of the opinion that within the two years, conditions all-round in Germany would have improved dramatically, and that all things being equal we would look at my future together and see what could be done. Both my parents had by now realized that I needed to pursue a path chosen by me. They felt that acquiring a second language could only be of advantage to me, as this was my main objective of applying for a position as an au pair in England.

Just before Christmas 1950 I left Germany for England, full of hope, and with my parents' best wishes, although my mother now had reservations. My destination was Southampton but I was met at Liverpool Street Station by Mr P. who spoke no German, and I realized in moments how difficult it would be to communicate. It was a long train journey punctuated by us pointing at various things in turn, trying to indicate that they were of interest. During the short taxi ride between stations in London I saw something of the vast devastation which had taken place during the war. It was strange for me to see it at first hand nearly five years after the war had ended. Somehow I had not been able to picture it as badly. My father had warned me that I might come up against some prejudice and advised me never to over-react. In fact his advice was sound. In the years I have lived in this country I have never openly encountered any prejudice for which I am very grateful, as I have had some very happy times here, especially in recent years.

And so I began a new life.

Elmers End — a Wartime Saga

by Irene Cropper

The elms were whispering when we came in spring of '44
And cautious rooks peered down at us, then greeted us with "C-A-W"
Our massive elms, the last of line, stood ninety feet or more;
I felt with them, affinity — a bond of love and awe.

I slept at night to soothing swish, as wind blew to and fro.
At morning's light those zany rooks flip-flapping soon would go.
'What happy chance had brought us here?' became my constant thought.
For every day I talked to them, such joy to me they brought.

In April though, I sensed a change, odd rumours on the breeze.
I heard no more that soothing swish, but moaning from the trees.
By night the elms looked sinister, foreboding trouble — change.
Rooks strutted close to us to feed, then squawked in manner strange.

"Whatever's wrong, dear rooks?" I cried: "You warn of ill, I know."
And answer made they quite distinct: caw caw! caw caw! go go!
"Why should we go? And where to then? — The States perhaps? And how?
September brings my unborn child. Why should we take flight now?"

But all through May the elmers groaned; it hurt to see their pain.
They frightened me so terribly — were bombs to drop again?
But all the news seemed better now — the Nazis on the run.
The war would surely end quite soon, for so said everyone.

Then in a flash our lives were changed: a June dawn, clear and bright.
Across the sky there came a whine — a 'thing' in endless flight.
And on and on, and on it came, in ever louder drone.
And then a silence — pause — a bang! Our hearts turned cold as stone.

"Has Jerry come?" our littlest said. "No pet," I tried to say.
But how explain I knew not what, when I could only pray?
And then again and then again for weeks and weeks on end.
It seemed that every flying bomb was aimed at Elmers End.

149

But fighter planes streaked here and there, to shoot the damn things down.
And barrage b'loons caught quite a few before they reached the town.
But houses cracked and ceilings fell, and windows blew with blast.
And squads of men worked round the clock to mend the damage fast.

We had to let the children go, with hundreds on the train.
We didn't even know where to, till they wrote home again.
"Oh God, please keep them safe," I prayed, "wherever they may be,
And find a kindly Christian soul who'll care for them, for me."

My prayer was heard: the angels smiled: to Gateshead sent them forth —
And found a home with folk we knew when we lived in the North!
September was approaching fast, and no one wanted me.
"Expectant mum? — Evacuate! — Book with the LCC!"

They packed me off to somewhere safe, in smug Northamptonshire:
A hostel just for pregnant mums: (the people thought it queer)
The women gave us dirty looks and whispered "prostitutes"
How could they know the hurt that gave, sequestered from our roots?

A touch of autumn tinged the trees when home again I went
To cope with bombs and new-born babe, to Elmers End in Kent.
I picked my way through glass-strewn streets, the gutters piled with rubble.
— South London in the last six weeks had had *its* share of trouble!

I found our house all boarded up, thick plaster dust within.
Some rooms had sheets of ersatz glass to let the daylight in.
But praise the Lord! the house still stood, the contents still intact.
The garden too was passing fair, but something vaguely lacked.

The elm trees seemed to sag and cry as if they mourned their dead.
And then it flashed upon my brain that all the rooks had fled.
They must have known of Hitler's plan, most devilish of all —
One never heard a V2's flight — one only heard the fall.

That winter was the saddest time, with bombs and rockets flying;
To blast dear London off the map mad Hitler kept on trying.
The elms seemed lost without their friends; I hardly saw a soul.
I missed the children and the rooks, and rockets claimed their toll.

Somehow the war had passed me by, though grim and not much fun.
Alas, a hundred yards away, they'd had a crazed V1.
It knocked the house and shelter down; inside were four or five.
But miracle of miracles! they'd all crawled out alive!

And then one dark December day I woke to hear "Caw Caw!"
And such a madding to and fro flip-flapping as before.
"The rooks are back! The rooks are back!" I shouted far and wide.
"It's safe to have the children home in time for Christmas-tide."

And so they came, with all the joy that only children bring.
So soon forgetting all the past, with promises of spring.
And now their friends the rooks were back, the elms regained their ease,
A-swishing, rustling singing sound, a whisp'ring in the breeze.

The rooks? They hardly noticed us: they squabbled without cease.
But neither did we notice them, we celebrated Peace.
My story is completely true: believe me if you can.
That rooks and elms reciprocate affinity with man.

'Yes, We have No Bananas'

by Olive Ainge (née Marney)

I think I must be amongst the youngest people who remember the beginning of the Second World War. I don't remember a great deal, as I was only 3 years 5 months old when it started, and as far as I was concerned, it was just there, we accepted it as normal. I found it hard to comprehend my mother's stories of shops bulging with bunches of bananas, and the popular song of, 'Yes, We have no Bananas' had no real significance for me; I HAD no bananas, but I didn't feel at all deprived.

It had been snowing on April 1st 1936, the day I was born, or so my mother tells me. My father was one of the many unemployed at the time, and 6 months later, with a job and a council house to tempt us, we left the quiet of rural Stowmarket and moved to the larger town of Ipswich. I have never seen the bungalow in which I spent those early days and all my childhood memories are of the area surrounding 242 Clapgate Lane, Ipswich in Suffolk. It amazes me that some people recall so much of their early years. I have only the most fragmented recollections of the world at the ages of 3 and 4, but at least I did begin to store up memories from when I was rising 5. My mother's fervent hope was that the war would be over before I started school, but this did not happen, and in 1941 I joined the group of other 5-year-olds under the kind and watchful eye of Miss Plum.

Miss Plum was a very calm lady, with a quiet voice and a rounded softness to her arms and cheeks that made me want to poke them with my finger. I never did of course, she kept too aloof for such familiarities. All of us children wore identity discs and so came my first mishap. My disc was on a short chain around my neck and pulling it forward with my thumbs to show my new friend, Valerie Brown, the chain snapped and the chilly necklace slid down to rest on top of my flannel liberty bodice. I was a chubby child and that liberty bodice, with its flat rubber buttons, must have added somewhat to my girth.

Valerie and I became firm friends, and I spent a lot of time in her home. Many years later, following the example of her elder sister, Barbara, she married an American and we lost touch. I do remember the strange fact though, with all the seemingly outlandish American surnames to which we became accustomed, Valerie married a Mr Brown! And so she never actually changed her name.

Another early school friend was Ronnie, a small fair-haired boy who had the distinction of living very close to the school. He was my very first sweetheart, and we became 'engaged' with a ring, made by my Uncle Franklin, of Aeroplane Glass. This was what we called the plastic used for plane windscreens. Uncle Franklin was always my favourite uncle and he and Auntie May, one of my mother's younger sisters, lived a few doors away with their sons, Noel and Brian, born just a year apart. I was six months younger than Noel and six months older than Brian, and when my father and uncle were 'called up' we spent even more time together. Uncle Franklin had been a cabinet-maker in civvy street and the bunks in the air raid shelter were very superior, with smooth edges and pleasing proportions. The entrance to the shelter faced that of their neighbours and they took it in turns to make tea for us all during the air raids. I looked forward to this because, unlike my mother, they used condensed milk which gave it, to my young palate, a very exotic flavour.

My brother Johnny was born in 1943, when I was nearly seven. One thing this meant was that for the first time we were entitled to a banana, when they were available. They were rationed to ½ a banana per child, so an only child had to go without. I tried very hard to make my sweet ration last a long time and in one instance I overdid it, and the sweets went mouldy. Fancy cakes were also few and far between but we did have little individual swiss rolls on special occasions and if, joy of joys, one of the soldier fathers came home on leave unexpectedly, we all cut off a slice from our cake to give him, and laughed to see that he ended up with more than the rest of us.

Occasionally we visited the other way round and took a picnic tea and Dad came out of camp for just a few hours. I remember we had jellies in jam-jars, which almost melted because the weather was so hot. I know I missed my Daddy a lot, and didn't really understand why he couldn't come home. In our living-room we had a large photograph of him in his Army uniform and I used to sing "We'll Meet Again" to it. It puzzled me at the time that my mother cried.

The first realization of the horror of war came when my friend Gloria was bombed. I turned a corner and saw a pile of rubble where I had been expecting to see her house. For a moment I thought I must have taken a wrong turning, then I knew I hadn't and that the home in which I had been so warmly welcomed was no more. By some miracle no one was seriously hurt.

I still loathe the sound of the air raid siren and remember vividly running down the garden in the dark to the shelter, with my mother clutching my baby brother in her arms. She had an old imitation crocodile skin handbag filled with small toys to keep him amused. As I got older I became more nervous and in my haste to reach the safety of the shelter one night, banged my head on the entrance. I was rather proud of my 'war wound' the next day. The V1 bombs, the 'Doodle-bugs', really frightened me and for a time I began to walk in my sleep.

Then it was over and we lit bonfires and some fathers came home and were demobbed. We tried to become a family again.

A Schoolboy's View

Not having to bear its responsibilities, children saw the war through different eyes from their elders. For boys at least it was a time of considerable excitement and absorbing interest, interspersed with occasional moments of fear, periods of tension, and the inevitable intervals of boredom. Only if and when their families were broken up by bombing, evacuation or military service, might children suffer the pangs of homesickness, loneliness, disorientation, or in the worst of cases, bereavement. Children are more resilient than adults. They accept life as it comes, and can quite enjoy the spectacle of disarray in the adult world, just as long as their family background remains fairly stable.

The war dominated everyone's life, of course, but if you grew up with war it did not seem a particularly abnormal state of affairs. Rather it was peace that was strange and difficult to comprehend. I remember how surprised I was to learn at the age of nine or ten that there were news broadcasts on the radio in peacetime. Until then I thought the evening news had been introduced solely for the purpose of reporting the war. I wondered what possible news you could have in peacetime. Peace was something of a puzzle.

One of the great benefits of the war for non-scholastic children in London were the frequent and prolonged closures of LCC schools. The implications of this for future adult life may not have been auspicious, but I imagine that few boys under the age of fourteen care to take a long-term view of life. If you were dependent on an LCC education and spent the whole war in London, the chances were that you enjoyed — if that's the word — only two uninterrupted years at school, in 1942 and 1943. The authorities tried to make up leeway by cutting school holidays to a miserly seven or ten days at Christmas and Easter and three weeks in summer. It did not help overmuch.

By the end of 44 half the 13-year-olds at the local school which I attended at this time, were as near illiterate as made no odds. Having to learn their tables by rote was not at all to the taste of young lads who had enjoyed years of freedom and licence in the streets or in far-flung rural areas. Boredom and frustration found expression at times in rebellious behaviour. Some boys refused to take the cane from masters, and the ensuing confrontations with school authority, with irate mothers occasionally joining in, made entertaining diversions from lessons. We hear much about classroom violence today and I do not profess to know how it compares with situations that I sometimes witnessed. I can say that I knew boys arrested before our eyes in the classroom and taken by the police, whither we knew not.

Among wartime sights to occupy a child's imagination were the huge barrage balloons that dotted the sky like flying silver fish. When I first saw them, which must have been at the time of Munich, they did seem to move quite rapidly in the sky. Of course, it was the clouds that moved. For a while I pondered on how it was that they scudded across the sky yet remained in the same place. When close hauled on the ground, however, they looked more like enormous stranded whales. Many a time we kids would stand to watch a balloon being winched down. The nearest balloon to where I lived was on Private Banks sportsground, by the corner of Catford Bridge and Canadian Avenue. Starting as a small remote object several thousand feet up, it slowly grew larger and more overpowering as it descended. At two hundred feet it was a huge billowing mass overshadowing the road. We waited, expectantly I must say, for a strong gust of wind to sweep it out of control at this critical point. The skill of the RAF handling crews seldom permitted fulfilment of our rather guilty hopes.

During a fierce thunderstorm in the summer of 40 the balloon located on playing fields in Randlesdown Road, Bellingham was struck by lightning and set on fire. It was a remarkable sight. Amid flashes of lightning and teeming rain, the burning beast strained in the low, black clouds like a maddened dog on the end of its leash. As the crew fought to lower it without causing it to crash in a blazing tangle among nearby properties, the balloon first veered over Bellingham Station, then went roaring off to the nether end of Brookhowse Road, only to return at a spanking rate of knots. The cable whined in the gusting wind, while pieces of fabric were ripped off and flapped away like injured birds. A large section fell in our front garden and we handed it over to the local warden. Sometimes the balloon was lost to view in the tempestuous clouds, only the flames being visible; at others it came swinging down as if bent on enveloping the nearest houses. It needed the brush of an artist to do justice to such surrealism.

Marching men of the REME were a regular sight in Catford. They were billeted in St. Dunstan's College, about two hundred of them I should say. Their work place was in Sangley Road, next to the Plaza Cinema, in what was for many years Dagenham Motors repair shops. Each morning and evening, and again at lunch-time, they tramped heavily in three ranks over Catford Bridge between billets and work place. I try to imagine what kind of traffic jam they would cause today on the South Circular Road. In the war years, however, motor traffic was very light — much lighter than in pre-war days — and by the time the troops wheeled into the college grounds only a couple of patient buses and a few cars would be bringing up the rear. They kept off the tram track, though I would not have cared to be in the outside rank as tramcars lurched past just inches away.

Many people look back with nostalgia to the old trams, yet they were not great favourites at the time. Everything inside seemed to be made of hard, angular cast iron, brass rails and handles. They lurched about in a most unexpected fashion. If you did not hang on tightly while climbing or descending the stairs you were liable to give yourself a nasty crack on the shins. They added a character to the main thoroughfares that is missing today. They were always getting stuck on the points outside Lewisham Town Hall (usually known as Catford Town Hall). Sometimes an electrical fault caused the driver's end to smoke and start to burn. Serious accidents could result from one tram running into another, and at least on one occasion during the war a tram run out of control to the bottom of Downham Way and overturned. The tracks were a constant hazard for cyclists. You needed to cross them at a good angle to avoid the front wheel getting jammed in the grooves. Forgetting this basic rule on one occasion, I was thrown bodily in the path of an oncoming army lorry. The lorry was only yards away and I had no time to ask for Divine intervention. I just closed my eyes. When I opened them the lorry had stopped about six feet from my head. The trams had character all right. Had it not been for the war they would have been replaced by trolley buses before 1943. Some already had been, although not those in Lewisham, Catford, or Forest Hill.

Speaking of transport, an experiment in the use of anthracite burners to save petrol was employed on the 36 bus route between West Kilburn and Hither Green. The burners looked like corrugated oil drums and were towed on two wheels by the buses. Each bus burned a ton of anthracite per week and needed refuelling every 80 miles. The burners were not really successful. What a struggle the 36 bus had to get up Sandhurst Road! I sometimes wondered whether the old puffer would make it to Torridon Road Library without everyone having to get out and push. Then there were some private cars converted to run on town gas stored in a balloon on top of the roof. An odd sight they made. This was not a very successful idea either.

Children made sacrifices for the war effort, don't think otherwise. I do not refer to soap rationing. Boys, at least, did not feel particularly deprived by that. Nor do I have in mind the rationing of sweets. We had a ration that varied between eight ounces and one pound per month. I've never had much of a sweet tooth, so one or two bars of chocolate a week seemed all right. Anyway, adults often gave up their sweet ration to children. Pretty decent of them really. We let them use our soap. Nasty chunks of the 'household' variety mostly. Toilet soap was thought a bit pansified and you did not get the same quantity for your ration. Loss of day trips or holidays to the coast, or anywhere else for that matter, did not bother me much, except perhaps on Bank Holidays when the heart yearned for a quick escape to all the fun of a seaside fairground, about which I had only read. But comics and boys' story papers — there was a sacrifice. Puny publications they were. Five short stories in the *Hotspur* and *Wizard* for twopence, instead of seven long stories found in fat pre-war copies. Worse, they came out fortnightly instead of weekly. Hard times. There were strict restrictions on the number of copies printed, so that if you did not get yours by about midday on the day of issue you might never find out what the boys of Red Circle School did next. Nowadays no child would read the long columns of close print that gave many of us pleasure. Plenty of pictures and the utmost economy in the written word is the order of today. Not that parents or teachers really approved of our reading such 'trash'. Young people seldom do anything that meets with their elders' approval.

I can recall clearly the occasion that low-level planes attacked the Lewisham area in January 1943. I was attending Adamsrill School, Sydenham at the time. We were just completing a singing lesson in the hall before taking lunch break at home when the sirens in Penge broke into our delicate rendering of Mendelssohn's 'On Wings of Song'. (How many 11-year-olds are taught that today?) I remember it because I thought afterwards how ironic that Nazi planes should interrupt us singing German music. But that was before I understood that Mendelssohn was a Jew. Anyway, we were still getting out of the hall when a lot of machine-gun fire broke out near at hand. Dog fights, I thought, remembering the Battle of Britain. Actually it was Sydenham gas works being gunned, among other places.

Those Adamsrill boys were real self-controlled gentlemen, for they stood back on the stairway to allow smaller children to go down to the basement shelter first. There was no pushing or shoving, let alone panic. I thought they were too good to be true. I'm sure those boys deserved to get on well in later life and I hope they have. The raid was practically over by the time we reached the basement. All the same, we had missed part of our cherished lunch break. All the boys were punctually back in class after lunch. except that, true to form, I was a few minutes late. Nothing was said but I felt a certain moral censure. Naturally, I thought they would *all* be late. Somewhat miffed, I told myself that I couldn't live up to their standards. It was not until later that day that we heard on the six o'clock news of the awful destruction of Sandhurst Road School. There but for the grace of God. . . .

We were bombed out of our home early in the 1940 blitz. Nothing unusual about that. Otherwise we were pretty lucky in this respect. Even the flying bombs gave our house a reasonably wide berth. The nearest fell 300 yards away. For part of the time during the V1 attacks I had a morning paper round. A distracted local newsagent asked me to deliver to Ravensbourne Park, Westdown Road, and a few other turnings because most of his regular delivery boys had very sensibly disappeared from the district. I can well remember popping *Daily Expresses* and *News Chronicles* through letter boxes while buzz bombs scuttled overhead among the clouds. Judging by a few complaints, they were not always the papers that had been ordered. No one seemed to regard it as out of the way for boys to be carrying out this useful function during the attacks . . . No ARP warden ever yelled at me to take cover. In fact, I hardly recall seeing a warden after the blitz. They were quite officious during the Battle of Britain, blowing their whistles and bawling at us when the sirens sounded. After that, I suppose they had too much else to do. Or perhaps they had given up as a bad job trying to train elements of the population in the basic precautions of survival.

To tell the truth, I eventually began to think that the buzz bombs were getting beyond a joke, so I volunteered to be evacuated to a safer part of the country.

I returned to Catford just as the V2 rocket bombardment was getting into its stride. I cannot say that I approved of this new-fangled remote-control warfare. Danger without excitement seemed to me the worst of all worlds. And the schools were back in business, making a determined effort to catch up on lost ground. You could not take shelter from the rockets because no warning was given of their approach. That being the case, the LCC probably reasoned that children might as well be killed while at school as when hanging around the streets. Some of us sat secondary school examinations in March 1945 amid pretty enormous explosions. I cannot be sure, but I think it may have been the day that Smithfield Market and Blackheath Village were hit. Somewhat to my surprise, I earned a grammar school place in all that commotion.

When the war ended a number of us boys went up to Blythe Hill Fields to get a panoramic view of the much-vaunted peacetime lights we had heard so much about in popular song. We could see a thin line of depressing blue lights in Brownhill Road and similar kinds of illumination stretching away in various directions. A dismal show I thought. Not a patch on searchlights. There were no neon signs; fuel economy forbade them and most were in desrepair anyway. Peacetime life seemed set to be as boring as we had suspected it might be. We were not young children any longer. A mysterious and rather seedy post-war world beckoned to us in our adolescence, and we contemplated the prospect with uncertainty and something less than total rapture.

The End of the War

Items taken from **The Times** *newspaper 3 July — 20 September 1945*

3rd July 1945

Winston Churchill was touring around showing himself to the people. He was a war hero, and because he had been such a good leader, everyone wanted to see him pass, and give him a cheer. The roads were lined with the London crowds, as he drove down the Kings Road, standing in the back of his car, and raising his two fingers in the Victory sign from time to time. He was obviously enjoying his popularity, and he must have expected to win the coming General Election. Everyone loved him — or so it seemed.

6th July 1945

A group of Army investigators established beyond doubt, that some men of the 2nd Special Air Service Regiment who had been dropped behind the German lines in the Vorges in France, had been captured and terribly tortured before being killed.

10th July 1945

The British liner, the *Ascanius*, had sailed for Haifa in Palestine from the port of Marseilles, with 808 Jewish people who had been recently released from the German concentration camps.

Field Marshal Sir Alexander was called to the War Office in London.

12th July 1945

Prisoners in Block 46 at Buchenwald Concentration camp were regularly used as 'guinea pigs', and dreadful experiments were carried out on them, under the instructions of the Berlin SS. When the victims became useless, they were inhumanely killed by phenol or prussic acid. Such was man's inhumanity to man. For this many Germans were put on trial, after investigations were carried out.

Mr De Valera created a sensation in the Dail when questioned, by declaring that Eire was really a Republic.

Commander of the 14th Army, General Sir William Slim, was welcomed at the Guildhall by the City of London. The country owed much to his gallant forces, who fought so courageously in the Burma Campaign.

13th July 1945

Lord Wavell, the Viceroy of India, was trying to keep the peace. He received Mr Jinnah, the leader of the Muslims, and Mr Gandhi at his house. There was disagreement between the Hindus and the Muslims, and the British did not want to leave India a divided country. The problem seemed to be whether India should be one country or two. Neither side would give in.

14th July 1945

The ships of the Canadian Pacific Line had transported over 750,000 servicemen and women across the water since the beginning of the war. Several of their boats had been torpedoed, and losses had been heavy.

17th July 1945

The great war leader, Field Marshal Montgomery arrived in Berlin on his way to attend the Three Powered Conference at Potsdam.

19th July 1945

Japan came under continuous attack from land, sea and air.

The Potsdam Conference got under way with the big three, Marshal Stalin, Winston Churchill and President Truman, all planning the end of the war, and how they would organize the peace.

The trial of the traitor Lord Haw-Haw, who was really William Joyce, was postponed for two months until the September Sessions. He was greatly hated in this country, because of his treacherous way of speaking over the German radio. There was a query whether he was born in England or America as he might have been able to avoid the ultimate end, had he been an American citizen.

25th July 1945

Work of reconstructing in the Netherlands was making great progress. Roads were being built, and the houses reconstructed.

Admiral Lord Louis Mountbatten, the Supreme Commander of South East Asia, was in London with his wife, Lady Edwina Mountbatten, and his eldest daughter Third Officer Patricia Mountbatten, WRNS.

Mr Churchill and Mr Attlee returned to London from Potsdam.

Marshal Pétain was on trial in Paris in the Palais de Justice, for betraying France. He had refused to answer the questions put to him, as he said, "I am heir to a catastrophe of which I was not the author." — He had been made the scapegoat, and had to comply.

27th July 1945

To the surprise of many people in the country, the Labour Party romped home at the General Election, and Clement Attlee became the leader of the new Government. Winston Churchill resigned.

30th July 1945

The magnificent 8th Army which had fought so hard through the Middle East and up through Italy, ceased to exist. The Lieutenant-General was Sir R.L. McCreery.

4th August 1945

Princess Elizabeth wearing the badge of a Junior Commander of the ATS for the first time, visited an MT Training Unit at Camberley, Surrey, where she had received her training.

The Potsdam Conference had decided upon the future of Germany. The country was to be divided into East and West Germany.

6th August 1945

The first atomic bomb was dropped on Hiroshima, obliterating 4 square miles of the city, and killing 53,000 people.

8th August 1945

Soviet Russia declared war on Japan; and a state of seige in Argentina was lifted.

9th August 1945

The Red Army invaded Manchuria, and the second atomic bomb was dropped on Nagasaki. Allied aircraft based at Okinawa destroyed 60 more Japanese ships. The Japanese Government announced their readiness to accept the Allied terms to surrender, providing the terms did not prejudice the prerogatives of the Emperor.

14th August 1945

The Japanese accepted the Allied terms.

15th August 1945

General Wingate's 'Chindit' Regiment of special airborne British and Indian troops was commended. Their activities behind the Japanese lines in Upper Burma helped to bring about a successful conclusion to the war.

15th August 1945

Marshal Pétain was sentenced to death, but as he was 89 the Court expressed a wish that the execution would not be carried out. The next day he was sent to a fortress, Le Pourtalet in the Pyrenees, and Madame Pétain was not allowed to go with him.

16th August 1945

King George VI asked for a National Day of Thanksgiving and Prayer, to be held in St. Paul's Cathedral on the next Sunday, 19th August.

General Eisenhower visited Moscow, and a great welcome was given to Field Marshal Montgomery when he drove through Lambeth.

General MacArthur ordered the Japanese to cease hostilities, and the war was over.

There were great Victory Day celebrations in London, and a State Opening of Parliament.

21st August 1945

Vidkun Quisling was put on trial in Norway for collaborating with the Germans, and the prosecution asked for the death sentence, because he had betrayed his country.

31st August 1945

The surrender of the Japanese was to be signed aboard the battleship the *Missouri* in Tokyo Bay.

7th September 1945

Poison gas no longer required, and not used as the Germans had refrained from using it, was dumped by sinking the ship *Empire Simba* off the coast of Western Ireland.

17th September 1945

The War trials of German war leaders was to open at Nuremberg. Hitler had avoided trial by killing himself, and so had Goebbels and Himmler.

The Battle of Britain pilots led by Group Captain Bader flew over London.

20th September 1945

The death sentence was passed on William Joyce.